EFFECTIVE BUSINESS WRITING
PRINCIPLES AND APPLICATIONS

EFFECTIVE BUSINESS WRITING
PRINCIPLES AND APPLICATIONS

Gerald William Morton
Auburn University at Montgomery

HARCOURT BRACE COLLEGE PUBLISHERS

Fort Worth   Philadelphia   San Diego   New York
Orlando   Austin   San Antonio
Toronto   London   Montreal   Sydney   Tokyo

iv

Publisher	*Ted Buchholz*
Editor in Chief	*Christopher P. Klein*
Acquisitions Editor	*Stephen T. Jordan / John P. Meyers*
Developmental Editor	*Michell Phifer*
Project Editor	*Betsy Cummings*
Production Manager	*Serena Barnett Manning*
Art Director	*Sue Hart*

ISBN: 0-15-501635-0

Library of Congress Catalog Card Number: 95-77299

Address for Editorial Correspondence: Harcourt Brace College Publishers, 301 Commerce Street, Suite 3700, Fort Worth, TX 76102.

Address for Orders: Harcourt Brace & Company, 6277 Sea Harbor Drive, Orlando, FL 32887-6777. 1-800-782-4479, or 1-800-433-0001 (in Florida).

Printed in the United States of America

5 6 7 8 9 0 1 2 3 4 066 0 9 8 7 6 5 4 3 2 1

For Kate

Preface

The teaching of business writing seems to be changing as rapidly as is the business technology that affects the process of communication. Students who take my classes today are well-skilled in using a technology that did not exist when I began teaching the course twenty years ago. We probably did not even imagine having access to such technology then. We have it now, however, and we must be prepared for the changes it has made in our students and in what business will expect from them when they graduate.

This said, however, it should also be said that much of what our students need has not changed. I am constantly aware of the fact that though they may command wonderful technological skills, their basic language skills are no less developed than were those of my students of the 1970s. This textbook offers an approach to the concepts and models important in business writing that begins with the basic tools of language—a strong vocabulary and effective sentence structure. Many of the textbooks currently available to business writing teachers pay too little attention to these matters. This book especially stresses the importance of students' learning to use verb-based language. The basic principles of style regarding verbs provide students with practical and usable guidelines that allow them to become better writers and editors.

This textbook proceeds from examining stylistic concerns at the sentence level to a discussion of reader, audience, and paragraph organization. Students are then asked to apply what they have learned about language to situations involving business writing. The emphasis of the book thereafter becomes application. Chapters 6-9 describing models of business writing discuss how the principles of language, organization, reader, and purpose can be applied to specific writing situations. The discussion and models include various types of memos, letters, resumés, and business reports.

A primary emphasis in this book is on product. Much of the excellent discussion of communication today stresses the process of writing. This book does not ignore the importance of process; the chapter on research is particularly structured to stress process. But business today is product oriented, and many of the documents we produce must be seen as just that, products. Writing a short memo cannot lead the writer into an extended process-oriented approach. Rather, the writer must be concerned with producing the most effective product possible in a short time.

I have been mindful while writing this book of what it does not do. It does not discuss new technologies, intercultural communication, or oral presentations. These are important matters which our students need to study, but they also need to command the material offered here. In particular, this book contains several features that make it helpful for students:

- three chapters on writing style
- a complete discussion of audience and purpose
- lengthy discussions of business letters and reports
- discussions of content and writing strategies for business documents
- editing exercises and student-generated writing assignments at the end of each chapter
- appendix material that includes student-written examples

Because this information is presented concisely, the book can stand alone or serve as a supplement.

At each stage of revision, the book has been class tested. The students have shown themselves to be fair, but demanding critics. The material that appears in this final version has received the most important review a project can enjoy: The review of those who are learning the principles and applications the book purports to teach. To all my students I am grateful. Not only have they assisted in the development of this text, they have, over the years, taught me essentially everything I know about how to teach writing.

Acknowledgments

This book would not have been possible were it not for those teachers and colleagues who have over the years coached me as I attempted to develop my own writing skills. I am especially grateful to Patrick Spurgeon, Percy Adams, Norman Sanders, and Alan Gribben. I have received considerable help in developing the text from others generous with their time and wise in their counsel. I particularly thank Michell Phifer, Betsy Cummings, and Stephen Jordan at Harcourt Brace. I shall always be grateful to Tom Ash, who kept telling me that the only way I would ever have a book I was willing to teach would be if I wrote it myself. Most important of all, however, I am grateful to Christen Wickham, whose desire to learn I could never match with a passion to teach. But as long as teachers have students like her, we have ample reason to continue with our efforts.

I would also like to thank the reviewers whose comments guided the manuscript through its various stages of development: Carol Pemberton, Normandale Community College; Wallace Coyle, Boston College; Richard Raspen, Wilkes University; Kim Ballard, Purdue University; Richard Kallan, University of California, Santa Barbara; Sally Ebest, University of St. Louis-Missouri.

Table of Contents

CHAPTER I

Using An Effective Vocabulary

Overview

*T*he purpose of this chapter is to review several basic concepts of language. Even though most of us have studied these concepts from the beginning of our formal education, certain fundamentals should never be far away. After all, the most architecturally sophisticated building rests on a foundation of concrete. If that foundation is flawed, then the integrity of the building is compromised. The same is true with our writing. When we appreciate the value of knowing language at its ground level, we are in a much better position to write effectively. The foundation upon which we build our sentences, paragraphs, memos, and reports will be solid. That foundation is the vocabulary we use.

Every concept in this chapter follows from a basic understanding of and appreciation for language. Our inherent assumption is that to write an effective report or letter, we must be able to write an effective paragraph; to write an effective paragraph, we must be able to write an effective sentence; to write effective sentences, we must use words effectively. Using words effectively means mastering a few basic vocabulary skills.

Developing an Effective Vocabulary

Rely on strong verbs to stress important ideas.

Use your strongest verb as the main verb in a sentence.

Avoid creating verbs from other parts of speech.

Distinguish between words that look and sound alike or have similar meanings.

Avoid padded phrases.

Use words according to their exact meanings.

Before continuing, let's try a simple test. Can you define the words *rebellion* and *revolution* so as to distinguish their meanings as they are used in political science? Both refer to political upheaval; both suggest, though they do not demand, violence. Both clearly refer to an adversarial situation. But they cannot be used interchangeably. *Rebellion* refers to an effort to replace the leader(s) of a given political order. *Revolution* refers to an effort to replace one existing political order with another. The distinction is significant. Consider how confusing a sentence would be to a reader who knows the distinction if the writer of the sentence does not use these words according to their precise meanings or uses them interchangeably. This example illustrates the point that effective writing begins with clear and precise command of words.

Now let's move to an example from the business world. Later in this text, we will look at a real-estate problem, along with a letter written in response to that problem. One of the crucial concepts in the situation will be the ability to distinguish the different meanings between the term *second mortgage* and the term *wrap mortgage*. The basic distinction is that a *wrap mortgage* involves a *second mortgage*, but it involves much more. To use these terms interchangeably would be a mistake. Such a mistake in usage would be as confusing to a reader in business as would the interchangeable use of *rebellion* and *revolution* to a reader in political science. As we look at this question of usage later, we will see the unfortunate results of the two terms' being used as if they mean the same thing.

Parts of Speech

Listing the parts of speech is easy. We learned them at an early age: noun, pronoun, verb, adjective, adverb, conjunction, preposition, and interjection. In professional writing the interjection—a word such as *ouch* or *oh*—would have no role because its sole purpose is to express elevated emotion. Such emotion blocks objective communication, so let's leave the interjection out as we consider the parts of speech.

The nouns and verbs are our principal parts of speech; they are the content words. And the verb is the word that expresses action or condition in a sentence, so it is generally more important than even the noun. From this concept, then, comes our first major principle of an effective vocabulary: *Effective writing begins with the use of strong verbs.* Writers who keep this concept in mind and write according to it will be better prepared to write effective professional memos, letters, and reports. However, because most writers tend to rely more heavily on nouns to express their ideas than they do on verbs, learning to use strong verbs may require breaking old habits and developing new ones.

To demonstrate how we can rely on different parts of speech to express important ideas, let's look at a series of example sentences that say basically the same thing. What makes these sentences different is their use of an adjective (believable), a noun (belief), or a verb (believe) to express an important idea:

Adjective

The chair of the personnel committee said he found **believable** the subcommittee's conclusion that a company day-care program would decrease absenteeism.

Noun

The chair of the personnel committee said he was of the **belief** that the subcommittee's conclusion that a company day-care program would decrease absenteeism was valid.

Verb

The chair of the personnel committee said he **believed** the subcommittee's conclusion that a company day-care program would decrease absenteeism.

The sentence using *believed* is so obviously preferable to the other two that we can easily see the value of relying on verbs to express important ideas. In fact, an editor revising the sentences that use *believable* and *belief* would write the sentence using *believed* without thinking about parts of speech, just about clarity. Let's look at one more example of the difference made by the part of speech we use to express an important idea. This example will use the noun (emphasis), the adjective (emphatic), and the verb (emphasize):

Adjective

The CEO was **emphatic** about his desire that the company increase its funding of new research.

Noun

The CEO gave **emphasis** to his desire that the company increase its funding of new research.

Verb

The CEO **emphasized** his desire that the company increase its funding of new research.

The sentence that uses the verb *emphasized* is clearly better than those using the noun and adjective to present the same idea. Even this sentence would be stronger were the writer to avoid the *ize* verb and simply use *stressed*. An effective editor would make this further revision to get the best possible verb. Again, an editor might not think in terms of parts of speech but rather note flaws in a sentence in a more general, but equally effective, manner. As we proceed through this text, however, we will look at parts of speech when discussing writing skills, particularly skills that allow us to use verbs effectively.

The Verb

Since the command of verbs is essential for a writer, we need to spend some time looking at the many roles verbs play in a sentence. Most importantly, the verb is the crucial word in the *predicate* of a sentence. We often avoid the term predicate and simply say *main verb* to refer to the action done by the subject of the sentence. Not all verbs express action, however. We also have the state-of-being verbs, or *linking verbs*, which establish a relationship between the subject of the sentence and an adjective or noun that follows the verb. The following sentence gives an example:

The report **is** too long for us to copy inexpensively.

The subject of the sentence is *report*, and the main verb is *is*. But *is* does not express an action. It connects the subject *report* with the adjective *long*, which describes the report. We have a complete sentence here, but no action is taking place because the main verb is a linking verb. Let's consider two more examples with a main linking verb:

It **is** obvious to most investors that current returns are poor.

Mr. Phillips **seems** to be the best candidate for the PR position.

The main verb of the first sentence is *is*, and that of the second is *seems*. In neither sentence does the main verb of the sentence express action, which may be a serious flaw if the idea in the sentence is concerned with action. Chapter III of this text will examine such flaws in detail.

Sometimes linking verbs are confused with passive voice verbs because the word *passive* suggests a lack of action. Linking verbs and passive voice verbs, however, are not at all related. The important distinction is between passive voice verbs and active voice verbs. We will thoroughly discuss this distinction later in the text. For now, let's simply look at an example of how a sentence can say essentially the same thing using either active or passive voice:

Active Voice

Several **members** of the committee **submitted** recommendations about how to improve the proposal.

Passive Voice

Recommendations about how to improve the proposal **were submitted** by several members of the committee.

In active voice, the subject, *members*, does the action of the main verb, *submitted*. In passive voice, the subject, *recommendations*, does not do the action of the main verb, *were submitted*, but rather receives that action. This distinction between active and passive voice is one every effective writer or editor needs to master.

The discussion of verbs thus far has dealt with the idea of a main verb in a sentence, the verb of the predicate. Verbs appear also in secondary roles and sometimes function as *nouns* or *modifiers*. These verbs appear in dependent clauses or phrases. In many respects, they are as important to strong writing as are the main verbs.

A verb in a dependent clause functions the same as does a verb in a main clause, except that it cannot be the predicate verb of a complete sentence. Consider the following sentence:

After the movie **ended,** Bob **decided** he **would stop** for a snack.

This sentence contains three verbs: *ended, decided,* and *would stop.* Only *decided* serves as a main verb because with its subject—*Bob decided*—we have a complete sentence. The other two verbs appear in dependent clauses and, thus, express secondary actions.

Also expressing secondary action are the phrases built from verbs: *participles, infinitives,* and *gerunds.* And like main verbs, these verb phrases can take objects, have voice, and express tense. Consider the following sentence:

> **Having been delayed** for weeks, the **meeting** was called by the CEO.

This sentence employs the secondary verb *delayed* as part of a participle phrase, *having been delayed.* The verb is in past tense and passive voice because the subject of the sentence—*meeting*—and here the *subject* of the secondary verb, did not do the *delaying.* It was the thing *delayed.* Notice what happens when we rewrite this sentence so both the main verb and the secondary verb are in active voice:

> **Having delayed** for weeks, the **CEO** called the meeting.

The shift in voice in this example creates a shift in emphasis as well. The first sentence stresses the word *meeting;* the second, the word *CEO.* The ability to determine emphasis is the reason the verb is so crucial to our writing. In a professional setting, decisions of emphasis are vital, and our writing must indicate our decisions.

The distinction between main verbs and secondary verbs has one significant application in our writing and gives us a second important principle of an effective vocabulary: *Use the main verb in a sentence to make an important point.* Sentences expressing an important point in a secondary verb and a minor point in the main verb need revision. The following example illustrates:

> It **is** crucial that the committee **submit** its day-care report before the next board meeting.

A good editor might notice several features of language in this sentence that need revision. The most significant feature, however, is the use of the unimportant verb *is* as the main verb and the important verb *submit* as the verb of a dependent clause. By revising the sentence so *submit* becomes the main verb of a sentence expressing the same thought, we would have:

The committee **must submit** its day-care report before the next board meeting.

The revised sentence is superior because the weak subject/verb structure, *it is*, is replaced by the stronger *committee must submit* as the main subject/verb combination. Later in this text we will look at other language features in this sentence that an editor would note. Even then, however, we will keep in mind the value of using the stronger verb effectively.

The writer's most important tool is the verb. Strong verbs convey meaning clearly. Weak ones obscure it. Throughout this text, we will return to this basic point. The student who feels that this brief review has not been sufficient should immediately seek help from a basic grammar text, a campus tutorial center, or the course instructor. Do not be afraid to admit a weakness on parts of speech. If you take a bit of time now to build on your foundation as a writer, you'll be pleased with the results later.

Nonverbs

As much as we benefit by understanding verbs and using them in our writing, we weaken our efforts when we use words as verbs that are actually other parts of speech. This tendency is pervasive today, not because writers are attempting to use verbs well, but rather because of overly loose vocabulary patterns. The following sentence gives an example of the problem:

Before we revise our employee benefits package, we need to see how the new government-mandated, family-leave program will affect our company by **conferencing** with our personnel staff.

In this sentence, the noun *conference* is used as a verb. The result is a stilted sentence, particularly to the reader who knows *conferencing* is a noun with a verb ending and is distracted by such usage. More to the point, the simple, direct verb *discussing* will convey the intended idea:

Before we revise our employee benefits package, we need to see how the new government-mandated, family-leave program will affect our company by **discussing** the matter with our personnel staff.

For one simple reason, the revised sentence is better. The predicate of the sentence is built on an actual verb, not a noun playing the role of a verb.

A second device too-often used to create verbs from other parts of speech is adding an *ize* ending to a noun, forming words such as *prioritize*, *creditize*, *minimize*, and *pluralize*. All these words have appeared in sentences. And sometimes some of them are effective; certainly *minimize* can be a useful word. But using *ize* words can become such a habit that our writing suffers as a result. The following sentence illustrates:

We will **creditize** your account to show this week's payments.

This sentence is not effective, primarily because the created verb *creditize* simply is not necessary. All the writer needs to say is:

We will **credit** this week's payments to your account.

This revised sentence teaches us a valuable lesson. In our effort to use verbs effectively, we should always appreciate the value of the simple verb, a verb such as *credit* in this revised sentence.

So much of the discussion in this textbook proceeds from the assumption that effective use of verbs enhances our writing that a brief warning is necessary. We should strive to use verbs, but not to the extent that we create them from other parts of speech or use them in places where those other parts of speech are preferable. Thus, we have our third principle of an effective vocabulary: *Do not use other parts of speech as verbs.*

Vocabulary Distinctions

Examine the following advertisement that appeared in a local newspaper a few years ago (the company name has been changed):

GRANNY'S HOME STYLE RESTAURANT

Specializing in Oldtime Cooking

Seven Locations to Conveniently Serve You

Were in Your Neighborhood

Consider what happened with this advertisement. One of its primary purposes was to let the public know that Granny's is conveniently located. And yet, the last line says just the opposite because the writer confused *were* and *we're*.

The English language is filled with words that look alike, sound alike, or have similar meanings. One of the most common language mistakes, as a result, is the confusion of these words. We all know to be careful with *there/their*, *to/too/two*, *affect/effect*, and *accept/except*. But what about *infer/imply*, *number/amount*, or *among/between*? Can you recognize the correct use of these words and avoid interchanging them? Too many pages would be required to discuss these and all the other pairs a writer might confuse. The point is that we never get past the need to consult a dictionary when we use a word with a look-alike, sound-alike, or similar-meaning *partner*. Even so, along the way we can pick up a few memory devices to help us with the more common pairs. For example, we might use the following devices to help us with important distinctions:

If you can count it, it's fewer; if not, it's less.

Stationery with an **e** means paper and **e**nvelopes.

Affect is a verb, for **a**ction; effect a noun (99 percent of the time).

The princi**pal** is your **pal**.

Be**tween two**; am**ong mo**re than two.

Perhaps this type of memory device is helpful to you; certainly you can work out your own. Again, the point is that we should never become so confident with our use of these words that we fail to pause and think twice when using them or to consult a dictionary if necessary to select the correct word.

In the Granny's Home Style Restaurant example, we see a mistake with language that a sympathetic reader will notice and probably enjoy as much as we did. Such a reader may not be confused, but will perhaps question the care with which the writer prepared the ad, leaving the writer's credibility in doubt. Such mistakes have a negative effect, even when they do not lead to confusion. Other mistakes with look-alike or sound-alike words do lead to confusion. Consider the following example:

The state must provide sufficient health-care funding to provide for its **emigrant** population.

This sentence appeared in a state funding document presented to a legislative committee. What it says, literally, is that the legislators should be prepared to fund health-care needs for citizens who have left the state. What it intended to say was that the state should provide sufficient funding to deal with a transient population. To say this, the sentence should have used *immigrant,* not *emigrant.* We are correct to question whether those reading the report would have understood what the writer meant and simply noticed the language mistake or whether they would have perceived the report to be recommending a level of funding sufficient to care for people who had left the state but might return to take advantage of health benefits. The potential for confusion certainly exists, and the example points again to the fact that writers must be careful when using words that look or sound alike or that have similar, but not identical, meanings. One final example will suggest even further how important a writer's care with such words can be. Consider in the following sentence which word (*its* or *it's*) conveys the intended meaning:

Every represented union must understand (**its/it's**) right to negotiate.

Actually, both would be appropriate, depending on what the writer wants to say. The reason both can work is that the word *right* can have two meanings in the sentence. It can mean *correct*, or it can mean *legal privilege*. The meaning of *right* depends on whether the writer uses the possessive pronoun *its* or uses the contraction *it's*. If the writer uses *its*, then the word *right* means *legal privilege*. If the writer uses *it's*, then *right* means *correct*. The writer's entire meaning depends, then, on the correct word choice. This example clearly points out the extent to which we can confuse our reader by careless usage. Better than any other example we might examine, it demonstrates the fourth principle of an effective vocabulary: *Correctly use words that look alike, sound alike, or have similar meanings.*

This entire discussion on vocabulary distinctions illustrates the degree to which effective writing begins with word choice. With the words we have been examining here, the writer has a clear *right* or *wrong* word selection. Sometimes the distinction between *right* and *wrong* word choice is not at issue but rather the distinction between a *better* or *poorer* word choice. The next two sections of this text look at vocabulary decisions that challenge us not so much to select the *right* word as they challenge us to select the *best* word.

Padded Phrases

Every professional knows that being economical is important, but being economical applies not just to money but to language as well. We should, therefore, discuss the types of habits writers develop that keep them from being economical with words. This discussion will give us a fifth important principle of an effective vocabulary: *Avoid the padded phrases that many writers use to sound "professional."* However, let's not confuse padded phrases with the technical language professionals sometimes need. The padded language we are discussing here is the language writers use when they want the reader not to see their meaning but rather to be impressed with their *professionalese.* This type of language is generally wordy, seldom clear, and always makes our writing sound like that of an undistinguished professional trying to hide meaning in a scheme of tired, old language instead of distinguishing him- or herself by using fresh and simple words. The following list illustrates the type of padded phrase we can eliminate:

Weak	Better
as per your request	as you requested
at a later point in time	later
at an earlier point in time	before
in the event that	if
considering the fact that	because
in addition to	also

We could all add to this list quickly because the inefficient use of language abounds in our society. When we examine this list, however, we quickly realize that the shorter words and phrases are much better. They allow the reader to deal with our ideas and not have to focus on the lengthy sentences we use to express them. The best way to appreciate the impact of such language, however, is to see it used in an extended example. The writer would want to revise the highlighted words:

MEMORANDUM

TO: All Office Personnel
FROM: Samuel Jones, Office Manager   *SJ*
DATE: January 19, 1996
RE: Parking Permits

In the event that you are not aware of the new parking-permit policies, I wish to outline those policies here. All office personnel **will be**

required to have a parking permit by January 23, 1996. **In addition to this requirement,** the permit must **be located in such a position that** our parking lot attendant will be able to see it. Any car in our lot without a permit will be towed. I am sorry that this policy is necessary, but **considering the fact that** so many people not employed in our office are using our lot, we must do something to be sure you have a space available.

Actually, this memo has much to recommend it. The tone is proper for the audience and situation, and the writer has been clear about what the policy demands and why. The padded phrases do, nonetheless, detract from the quality of the writing. A revised version of the memo will demonstrate this fact:

MEMORANDUM

TO: All Office Personnel

FROM: Samuel Jones, Office Manager *SJ*

DATE: January 19, 1996

RE: Parking Permits

If you are not aware of the new parking-permit policies, I wish to outline those policies here. All office personnel **must** have a parking permit by January 23, 1996. **Also,** the permit must **be visible to** our parking lot attendant. Any car in our lot without a permit will be towed. I am sorry that this policy is necessary, but **because** so many people not employed in our office are using our lot, we must do something to be sure you have a space available.

The few changes made in this revised memo contribute to its effectiveness in one simple way. The direct and efficient vocabulary enhances the writer's other positive decisions about tone and content. This memo does not have overused and padded phrases. Rather, the language is simple, crisp, and direct. The reader can, therefore, concentrate on the message without being distracted by the words used to present it.

Precision

This chapter on vocabulary began by discussing the need to use words according to their exact meaning. The examples used were the terms from political science, *rebellion* and *revolution,* and those from business, *second mortgage* and *wrap mortgage.* The simple fact is that language is a tool for precision. Words have specific meanings and must be used according to those meanings. A writer should never settle for a word that *is close to the necessary meaning.* Effective writing depends on the writer's always using the best, the most exact, word to convey an idea. Actually, both the writer and reader have a responsibility here. Both must use and understand words according to their dictionary meaning, not necessarily the meaning they sometimes acquire by careless usage in society (such as on television or in "cute" advertising).

The following memorandum provides an excellent example of what happens when words are not used according to their exact meanings. The highlighted words best illustrate the problem:

MEMORANDUM

TO: John Phillips, Personnel Director

FROM: Jane Simpson, Director of Public Relations

DATE: August 23, 1996

RE: Assistant PR Director

Due to the fact that you have approved my proposal that we promote a member of my staff to Assistant Director of Public Relations, I wish to recommend the employee whose job skills and potential best **portray** that of an efficient and effective supervisor. Specifically, I recommend that Ann Levis receive the promotion.

Ann's primary responsibility since we hired her has been to prepare company brochures and pamphlets. Her ability to work **across** the different departments of the company in preparing this material **expresses** her ability to communicate with colleagues. Her degrees in advertising and English, along with seven years in public relations, **convey** her grasp of the advertising industry and **intuitiveness of the communicating process.** She has excelled in company training seminars. However, the **most substantial** basis of my recommendation is her demonstrated ability as a decision-maker.

I appreciate your considering my suggestion and look forward to hearing from you.

Now let's consider how much more effective this memo is if the highlighted language is changed:

MEMORANDUM

TO:	John Phillips, Personnel Director
FROM:	Jane Simpson, Director of Public Relations
DATE:	August 23, 1996
RE:	Assistant PR Director

Because you have approved my proposal that we promote a member of my staff to Assistant Director of Public Relations, I wish to recommend the employee whose job skills and potential best **parallel those** of an efficient and effective supervisor. Specifically, I recommend that Ann Levis receive the promotion.

Ann's primary responsibility since we hired her has been to prepare company brochures and pamphlets. Her ability to work **with** the different departments of the company in preparing this material **demonstrates** her ability to communicate with colleagues. Her degrees in advertising and English, along with seven years in public relations, **suggest** her grasp of the advertising industry and **command of the communication process.** She has excelled in company training seminars. However, the **primary** basis of my recommendation is her demonstrated ability as a decision-maker.

I appreciate your considering my suggestion and look forward to hearing from you.

The highlighted language in this revised memo indicates the changes that make a difference. While the reader of the first memo will no doubt get the general message the writer is presenting, that reader will also find the imprecise language a nuisance. The simple changes in the second memo allow the reader to concentrate on the content of the memo without distraction. These revisions give us a sixth principle of an effective vocabulary: *Use words according to their precise meanings.*

Summary

Throughout this first chapter, we have looked at the importance of a clear and precise vocabulary. A review of major points follows:

Developing an Effective Vocabulary

Rely on strong verbs to stress important ideas.

Use your strongest verb as the main verb in a sentence.

Avoid creating verbs from other parts of speech.

Distinguish between words that look and sound alike or have similar meanings.

Avoid padded phrases.

Use words according to their exact meanings.

The writer who follows these basic vocabulary guidelines will have a strong foundation for writing effective memos, letters, and reports.

Exercises

I. **Identifying Verbs:**   Study the following sentences, list the verbs and verb phrases, and then determine whether they are main verbs or secondary verbs. Also indicate any linking verbs. Finally, decide whether the verbs are in active or passive voice.

1.   After our repeated attempts at solving the marketing problem, ACME's CEO decided to hire a forecasting consultant to examine the situation.

2.   The discussion about benefits having been delayed twice, we are in the process of calling in help from the union.

3.   For the pressing problem of cash flow to be resolved, the company will need to reduce its salaried employees by 20 percent over the next few months.

4.   Industry standards for steel must be established based on current construction needs and the research that has been produced since the last review.

5.   A major problem with the environment is the ever-increasing volume of CO_2 emissions allowed by government.

II.   **Vocabulary Distinctions:**   Read the following sentences, use your dictionary, and correct any vocabulary errors that result from confusion of look-alike/sound-alike words or words with similar meanings.

1.   Before proceeding, we will need to determine whether increased advertising will be an affective means of increasing sales.

2.   I was sure that in his memo the office manager was inferring that everyone in the office was guilty of taking excessive time at lunch.

3.   Most of the new employees indicated that their ready to train on the new computer system.

4. Every expert on the ozone problem I have read has a different opinion; with this disagreement between experts, how can politicians structure proper legislation.

5. If we continue to loose topsoil at the current rate, this field will be a total lose by the end of the decade.

6. As soon as you determine the affect of the new EPA standards on our production capacity, prepare a report for the board of directors.

7. At the moment, the company is facing to many government restrictions to generate much increase in revenues.

8. At present levels, the amount of units we are producing per hour is less than needed to meet our existing orders.

9. The committee's report indicated that it's main problem was getting information.

10. According to most experts, a family-leave plan that adds compensated leave to the government-required 12 weeks of uncompensated leave will illicit favorable responses from most employees and contribute to their moral.

11. After I read the proposal, I was convinced that we should adapt all its provisions accept the forth, which seemed not consistent with other company policies.

12. Let's be sure that all perspective transfers are told that if they are sent to the Jonestown plant, the company will provide all their moving expenses.

13. Probably the only way to lesson our high absenteeism rate is to assist parents with the day-care problems that have resulted from the closing of the Kidscare School.

14. Before we will be able to run this program, were going to have to excess the reserve memory in our system.

15. The new CEO offered this advise; supervisors will deal with all routine matters, and division heads must be free to work on innovative ways to enhance productivity.

III. **Padded Phrases:**   Rewrite the following sentences to remove the padded phrases.

1. In the event that the production report does not arrive on time, you need to be prepared to delay the discussion.

2. If we delay that discussion until a later point in time, we will have to be sure that no one objects.

3. In the event that even one member of the board insists that we proceed, we will report on the basis of the last production reports.

4. Considering the fact that I don't expect such a request, we are probably safe.

5. As per the board's request, however, I want you to be prepared.

6. The company will be spending somewhere in the neighborhood of $25,000 to fund the first stage of the proposed reorganization plan.

7. I am of the opinion that the only way to enhance morale is by restructuring the current sick-leave provisions in the employees' benefits package.

8.   At such a point in time that the board approves the new position, we will begin a national search to find a superior candidate.

9.   In order that our supervisors can become more aware of the problem of sexual harassment, we have scheduled a training seminar with an attorney who handles discrimination cases.

10.   The audit proved that in addition to our standard deductions for business expenses, we should consider sheltering some funds in capital investment.

IV.   **Precise Usage:**   Edit the following sentences to replace words that do not convey the intended meaning. You may need to use the context of the sentence to be sure of your revisions. Consult a dictionary when you are unsure about a change you wish to make.

1.   For the moment, let's replace the leave policy we've been using for the one that the board will be voting on at its next meeting.

2.   If you will be at the directors' meeting next week, I'll ask that you convey my committee's report since I can't attend.

3.   No one likes the company's current leave policy, but let me insist that many companies our size don't even have one.

4.   Subsection C of Item 4 in the contract is completely misleading, so I plan to offer several attachments to see if we can't clarify its meaning.

5.   Before I sign this contract, I want an accountant who can discuss those sections I don't understand.

6. Given the board's current conservative nature, I'm going to the meeting prepared to debate the company's need for compensated maternity leave.

7. If my presence at the union meeting will reinforce the membership during the contract vote, then I'll be there.

8. When I told my supervisor about the problems we're having with the trainees, he was very genteel and suggested he meet with them next week.

9. We need 12 reproductions of the leasing agreement before we meet with the attorneys.

10. I'm tired of fighting the red tape on my claim. Can someone point me to the person who can resolve the delays?

V. **Editing:**   Revise the following paragraph to eliminate any of the vocabulary problems discussed in this chapter. You should use a dictionary whenever you need to check the precise meaning of a word used in the paragraph or one you wish to use but are not sure about.

After the meeting ended, several board members were of the opinion that their had been inadequate discussion of the new marketing campaign. One frustrated member said the chair's abruptly ending the discussion inferred that the campaign would proceed irregardless of the concerns that had been voiced. No less than four members questioned whether the chair should continue heading the board and indicated that at a later point in time they might impose a challenge to his continuing in his position. The frustration was not limited, however, to the way in which the meeting was conducted but to the marketing campaign as well. For the reason that the campaign does not maximize the company's public-service commitment, some members thought that a primary opportunity to generate good will was being forgotten. As one board member stated, finding several opinions between the members about how to promote the company's products is easy, but everyone is in agreement about the need to promote the company as a good neighbor. Clearly, the next meeting of the board will be interesting as the marketing strategy and possibly the chair come under attack.

CHAPTER
11

Effective Use of Verbs

Overview

A significant part of the first chapter in this textbook discussed the importance of using verbs effectively in our writing. In this chapter, we will examine ways to do just that. Specifically, we will study four principles of using verbs to create a verb-based writing style. A verb-based style means:

Verb-based Style

The main action in a sentence should be expressed in a verb, as opposed to a noun or modifier.

Sentences should use strong verbs that do not need adverb modifiers.

Verbs should generally be in active voice.

Linking verbs should be used sparingly as main verbs.

Of all the qualities an effective writing style should have, the use of strong, active voice verbs to express the primary action in a sentence is the most important.

Using Verbs Instead of Nouns

The strongest part of speech is the verb. However, our language is such that many words can serve as either verbs or nouns, depending on how they appear in a sentence. The word *use*, for example, can be both verb or noun, as can the word *writing*. More common is the use of nouns created from verbs, as when *demonstrate* becomes *demonstration* or *retire* becomes *retirement*. In fact, most nouns that end in *ion* or *ment* are built from verbs. Because readers are more likely to retain ideas presented through verbs, however, sentences that use such nouns will be more effective if they are rewritten to use verbs instead. A series of examples will illustrate this fact:

Weak

We will want you to give a **discussion** of FASB 87 at the next workshop.

Revised

We will want you to **discuss** FASB 87 at the next workshop.

The primary idea here, what the writer is talking about, is presented in the word *discussion* in the weak sentence. But *discussion* is a noun, which means that the main idea is not presented in the strongest part of speech. The primary point in the sentence is what the writer wants the reader to do. The revised sentence stresses this point because it appears in the verb *discuss*. A second example is particularly interesting because it changes four commonly used nouns to verbs:

Weak

In order to provide **motivation** for our clients to keep accurate records when we do their tax **preparation,** we have developed a brochure that gives a **description** of what you need for expense **documentation.**

Revised

In order to **motivate** our clients to keep accurate records when we **prepare** their taxes, we have developed a brochure **describing** what you need to **document** expenses.

Nouns such as *motivation, preparation, description,* and *documentation* are perfectly acceptable words. Yet, the revised sentence, which turns these nouns into the verbs *motivate, prepare, describe,* and *document,* is decidedly better. It is shorter and more direct. Most important, readers can better remember the ideas presented in a sentence when those ideas are presented in verbs rather than another part of speech. In this sentence, that means remembering what the accountant needs.

Before continuing to a second method for using verbs effectively, let's look at an extended example of writing that relies too heavily on the use of weak nouns:

MEMORANDUM

TO: Ms. Janet Frosh

FROM: David Harlen, Human Resources Director

DATE: July 23, 1996   *DH*

RE: Employee of the Year Award

You are aware of your supervisor's **nomination** of you for the Jones Retailers Employee of the Year award. You have my **congratulations** for that **nomination.** I can now inform you that the committee **tasked** with the **review** of those **nominations** has reached the **end** of its work and presented its **recommendation** for that award. Although many employees were considered, I am pleased to say that the committee found your **nomination** particularly deserved. You have, therefore, been named the Jones Retailer Employee of the Year and will receive your public **recognition** at the annual Holiday Banquet. I shall be in touch about the details for making this award. For now, please accept my **congratulations** for this **recognition** of your service to the company.

This memo provides an excellent example of what happens to our style when we rely too heavily on nouns. This memo uses nouns— *nomination, recommendation, recognition, review, end, congratulations*— to make almost every important point. The result is a dry, objective tone in a memo that gives an employee good news. Tone in writing means the way our messages sound because of the language and sentence structure we use. It is often a difficult-to-control characteristic of our writing. The memo here should have a warmer tone so the employee feels that the award is meaningful. The tone, however, is so cold that Ms. Frosh might be rather confused, instead of surprised in a delightful way, when she finally realizes that she has received the award. Consider how simply shifting to a verb-based style would remedy this problem:

MEMORANDUM

TO: Ms. Janet Frosh

FROM: David Harlen, Human Resources Director

DATE: July 23, 1996   *DH*

RE: Employee of the Year Award

You are aware that your supervisor **has nominated** you for the Jones Retailers Employee of the Year award. I **congratulate** you for this achievement. I am pleased to inform you that the committee **reviewing** these nominations **has completed** its work and **has recommended** that you receive this award. You have, therefore, been named the Jones Retailer Employee of the Year and will **be recognized** publicly at the annual Holiday Banquet. I shall be in touch about the details for making this award. For now, allow me again to **congratulate** you that your co-workers **have recognized** your service to the company.

This memo might still be stronger with certain content revisions, but the shift away from nouns to verbs has at the very least created the crisper style and warmer tone such good news deserves. Fortunately, our language allows us the option of using verbs instead of nouns to express our thoughts.

Using Strong Verbs

Not only do writers want to use verbs to express main ideas, but also they want to use the strongest verbs available. Unfortunately, most of us tend to write as we speak, which means we rely on the limited vocabulary we use when we are thinking and speaking at the same time. This habit means we use only a small number of words that come quickly to mind, particularly weak verbs with adverbs to clarify them. A better approach to take when writing is to rely on stronger verbs that need no modifiers and that express our ideas more forcefully. Consider the following list of verb/adverb phrases and the strong verbs that can replace them:

Verb Phrase	Strong Verb
look over	review
look very closely at	examine
read back over	reread
run very quickly	sprint
spoke quite clearly	articulated

Words such as *sprint* and *examine* create a more vivid mental picture for the reader than do phrases such as *run very quickly* and *look very closely at*. This vivid mental picture encourages the reader to retain the ideas presented by the strong verbs. Let's look at a sentence that uses a weak verb phrase and then at a revision of that sentence using a strong verb to create a mental picture:

Weak

Everyone involved with ACME Incorporated's taxes will need to **look very carefully at** its subsidiary restructuring plans.

Revised

Everyone involved with ACME Incorporated's taxes will need to **examine** its subsidiary restructuring plans.

The revised sentence uses the strong verb *examine* to give the accountants their instructions. We can look at things with varying degrees of attention; the writer originally uses *carefully* to stress the attention necessary in this situation. The revised verb makes clear that the readers must be careful—the writer doesn't need the modifier *carefully* to stress the point.

Avoiding Passive Voice Verbs

Everyone who has taken a writing course has heard the advice: *Avoid passive voice verbs.* Yet, one of the most common flaws in writing is the use of such verbs. Many people may use passive voice verbs because they do not understand the difference between those verbs and their active voice counterparts. They may use such verbs because they want the effect produced by passive voice. Sometimes, in fact, passive voice produces precisely the effect a writer may want. However, these situations are the exception, not the rule.

Let's begin with a review of what passive voice does and does not mean:

Passive Voice

Does not mean a nonaction verb

Does not mean a verb expressing past action

Does mean a verb that expresses action done **to** not **by** its subject

---

In most cases, the active voice verb creates better emphasis by presenting ideas in the order readers need them. A psychologist would say that active voice verbs assist our encoding of information. On a less technical level, what we need to realize is that they sound better and help writers make their points.

First, let's look at the distinction between active and passive voice in sentences that say the same thing but have different subject/verb relationships:

Active Voice

Several members of the committee **submitted** recommendations about how to improve the proposal.

Passive Voice

Recommendations about how to improve the proposal **were submitted** by several members of the committee.

The sentences say the same thing, but what is important is that the emphasis is different. The different emphasis affects the reader's ability to determine the writer's main point. The subject—the word stressed—in active voice is *members*. The emphasis on *members* is proper, given that they are the ones who made the recommendations. But in passive voice, the stressed word is *recommendations*. The *recommendations* performed no action and, therefore, should not be the crucial word in the sentence. Such an emphasis simply does not make sense if the sentence centers on the action of submitting.

Active voice verbs stress the doer of the action expressed in a sentence. Passive voice verbs stress who or what receives the action or has the action done to it. Again, some sentences work better with passive voice, but rarely is the emphasis created by passive voice more appropriate than the emphasis created by active voice. This point is so important that we need to look at our last example sentences again:

Active Voice

Several members of the committee **submitted** recommendations about how to improve the proposal.

Passive Voice

Recommendations about how to improve the proposal **were submitted** by several members of the committee.

Notice the direction of the example sentence as it moves from *who* did *what* to *whom*. In active voice, this movement goes from the beginning of the sentence to the end, from *members* to *submitted* to *recommendations.* In passive voice, this movement goes from the end to the beginning.

Now consider the analogy of the human mind as a computer. Active voice sentences enter information into that computer in an order that can be understood. In passive voice, however, we need another program, one that reconfigures the information to a format we can work with. This is in essence what happens when we read passive voice sentences, and the extra step can cause us to lose part of the information. Let's look at another example:

Weak

The audit **might have been avoided** by the company if the tax accountants had been given enough time to review the new policies.

Revised

The company **might have avoided** the audit if the tax accountants had had enough time to review the new policies.

The rambling sentence structure of the first sentence leaves the reader uncertain what the main point really is. And yet, when we change the verb, and the sentence re-forms around it, we have, *The company might have avoided the audit* . . . . Notice how this sentence really gets to the point because the verb is in active voice.

One final comment about passive voice is in order. Often, passive voice appears in sentences that have other problems—problems with *it* and *there* subjects (see Chapter III) and weak nouns. Sentences with two or more such problems really struggle to make their point. Consider the following example:

Weak

There **have been established** five new programs by our forecasting consultant for predicting market conditions.

Revised

Our forecasting consultant **has established** five new programs for predicting market conditions.

The combination of the *there* subject and the passive voice verb *have been established* in the weak sentence has one major negative effect. The key idea of *forecasting consultant* gets lost in the middle of a rambling sentence—lost in the structure and lost to the reader. We see a similar situation in the following example:

Weak

It **has been indicated** by our analysis that the new policies for prorating business expenses will cost the company between $1 million and $1.5 million.

Revised

Our analysis **indicates** that the new policies for prorating business expenses will cost the company between $1 million and $1.5 million.

Again, the revised sentence is better. Getting the words *analysis indicates* to the front of the sentence makes a real difference. Probably what has happened here is that the writer has not really come to terms with the idea he or she is presenting. If that idea is fuzzy to the writer, then it will be fuzzy on paper. This being the case, writing and editing for the problems we have covered thus far can become a way of thinking through ideas. When they are clear in our minds, they are probably also clear on paper.

Although active voice verbs are better than passive voice verbs in most situations, passive voice does have a role to play in our writing. We will see in Chapter IV that passive voice allows us to rewrite sentences that are gender specific so they become gender neutral. This is one positive use of passive voice. Another appears in process or procedure writing, when who does the specific actions being documented is unimportant. In such situations, the writer can use passive voice to stress the process itself. The following example illustrates:

Weak

Before **introducing** any nonauthorized software to the company's computer system, employees **must have** it approved by the systems director.

Revised

Nonauthorized software must **be approved** by the systems director before **being introduced** to the company's computer system.

The weak sentence uses an active voice participle, *introducing,* and an active voice main verb, *must have.* The subject of this sentence is *employees.* This subject creates improper emphasis because what the sentence is actually dealing with is *nonauthorized software.* By shifting to passive voice, the writer can generate this emphasis. The revised sentence makes this shift by making *nonauthorized software* the subject. Now the emphasis is proper for the writer's actual topic.

Such a shift in emphasis made possible by a shift in voice also will serve a writer well in other situations. Consider the following example:

Weak

I have **completed** a review of your recent complaint but found no fault with Phifer and Associates' procedures.

Revised

A review of your complaint **has been completed** but indicates no fault with Phifer and Associates' procedures.

In order to use active voice, the weak sentence also uses the first-person subject *I.* First person can be very effective at times but not in this example sentence. Here it makes the writer, not the review of the complaint, the focus. A shift into passive voice with the verb *has been completed* also creates a subject shift, making *review* the primary focus of the sentence. Such use of passive voice can be especially helpful in many professional situations, as we will see in Chapter VI, which deals with business letters.

Linking Verbs as Main Verbs

Because verbs are the words in a sentence which usually convey the most important information, a writer must take care to be sure that the main verb, in particular, is as strong as possible. Generally, therefore, we should avoid using linking verbs as main verbs. They express no action and convey little meaning. Linking verbs serve little more than a grammatical function, and sentences that use them as main verbs are generally stronger when rewritten. Consider the following example:

Weak

The foreman **has** several complaints he received about our handling of the ACE, Inc., order.

Revised

The foreman **received** several complaints about our handling of the ACE, Inc., order.

Revising this weak sentence simply means taking the verb from the dependent clause and making it the main verb in the sentence. The following example is similar:

Weak

There **are** several qualified candidates who **have applied** for the public relations position.

Revised

Several qualified candidates **have applied** for the public relations position.

Again, the revision is simple, but it allows the sentence to take as its main verb *have applied* instead of the weak linking verb *are*. Linking verbs do, of course, have their place in our writing, but the writer who limits the use of such verbs will have a stronger prose style than the writer who does not employ strong, active voice verbs and who frequently uses linking verbs as main verbs.

Summary

The best way to review the importance of using strong verbs will be to examine and then revise a paragraph that does not use them. The problems in the paragraph appear in bold print:

It has been the **decision** of the review committee to cite violations of safety standards in Department A. A concern with these violations **was indicated** by the department supervisor, but it **was** the opinion of the committee members that a formal notice **was** appropriate. The committee members **were** also of the opinion that **utilization** of a regular review visit to Department A **to look very closely at** the progress on recommended improvements was necessary. The department supervisor gave an **indication** of his **agreement** to those review visits.

By editing this paragraph to improve the verbs, we can revise the material to produce a much clearer prose that stresses all the important points. The new subject/verb structures in the revised paragraph appear in bold print to show the most important changes:

The review **committee has decided** to cite violations of safety standards in Department A. Although the **department supervisor has indicated** his concern with these problems, the **committee members felt** that a formal notice was appropriate. The **committee saw** also a need for regular review visits to Department A **to examine** the progress on recommended improvements. The **department supervisor indicated** he **agreed** with those review visits.

The revised paragraph is significantly improved. The subjects of the sentences are important words such as *review committee* and *supervisor*. Nouns such as *decision, utilization,* and *indication* have become verbs. And the verbs are in active voice. These changes allow the paragraph to stress its important ideas so the reader can see exactly what the writer intends to say.

Revisions resulting from an emphasis on strong verbs are significant. Again, the four basic principles of a verb-based style are:

Verb-based Style

The main action in a sentence should be expressed in a verb as opposed to a noun or modifier.

Sentences should use strong verbs that do not need adverb modifiers.

Verbs generally should be in active voice.

Linking verbs should be used sparingly as main verbs.

Following these principles can make a significant difference in the quality of writing we produce.

Exercises

I. **Using Verbs Instead of Nouns:** Rewrite the following sentences to remove nouns by turning those nouns into strong verbs.

    1. The CEO gave the indication that he would step down if the board asked him to do so.

2.   Perhaps the best sign that the economy is experiencing some improvement is the level of Christmas sales we have seen.

3.   You need to be completed with your preparation for the meeting well in advance so we can discuss our strategy for selling the proposal.

4.   It is my belief that we can cut costs by 10 percent if we go with a different supplier.

5.   I want you to place emphasis on the ROI grain futures will offer in the short term.

6.   I offered my recommendation for Jones because he has never failed to complete a project for me.

7.   If we can complete the development of the X-10 by 1994, we will again be able to compete with ACE, Inc., for government contracts.

8.   Jones made a poor distinction between the X-10 and the X-10A when he gave his presentation.

9.   No one is sure of what use we can make of an intern, but we'd like to look into placing one and helping the school with its preprofessional training program.

10.   The personnel director has begun his investigation of the large turnover at the Dadeville plant.

II.   **Verb-Based Language:**   Rewrite the following sentences so they use verbs to full advantage.

1.   The decision was made by management to look back over each bid before awarding the contract.

2.   There have been seven bids that the company has rejected as not meeting the contract requirements.

3.   Every effort was made by the forecaster to account for the variables that might affect production.

4.   The contract having been awarded, the decision was made by the CEO to meet immediately with the contract supervisor.

5.   Every attempt at negotiation having been rejected by the union, we simply moved ahead with the lockout.

6.   Seven new safety policies were mandated by ASO.

7.   Each month we seem to be confronted with a sexual harassment charge against one of our chief executives.

8.   A family-leave plan will be part of the discussion at the next board meeting.

9.   There are several applicants who have qualified for a promotion.

10.   Any decision about increasing taxes will not be made by this administration until after consulting with leaders from both parties.

III.   Editing for Strong Verbs: Rewrite the following paragraph to use stronger verbs.

An investigation of the new IRS guidelines for deductible business expenses has been conducted by several members of the Tax Department, and some important changes in the code have been identified. It is their belief that some of our smaller clients may enjoy some benefit from the changes, but that these changes will provide no relief from tax burden for our larger clients. It has further been determined by these members of our staff that providing documentation for deductible expenses will become more difficult. To outline the important items in the new IRS code, a workshop will be given by the head of the Tax Department next Friday morning at 9 a.m. It should be your plan to attend this important meeting.

IV. **Using Strong Passive Voice Verbs:** Select as your topic a process with which you are comfortable. You might select balancing a checkbook, creating a spreadsheet with a specific software package, or researching a topic in your school library. Write the steps in this process using only active voice verbs. Then rewrite those steps in sentences that use passive voice verbs. Notice the shift in emphasis and decide which you prefer.

CHAPTER III

Writing Effective Sentences

Overview

A writer who has mastered the vocabulary skills discussed in the first two chapters of this text will be well on the way to writing effective sentences. Sentences are, after all, composed of words and draw much of their strength from a writer's clear and precise vocabulary. Especially important to writing clear sentences are the verb skills stressed in Chapter II. Not all sentence-structure flaws are the result of poor verbs, so we need to look at other sentence-structure skills as well.

Let's begin with a basic understanding of what a sentence is and what it should do to be effective. First, most sentences need to have one fundamental objective; they should make one main point. When a sentence attempts to make more than one main point, the writer risks interfering with the reader's understanding of what the sentence is really trying to say.

Second, sentences that do need to make more than one point generally should state one primary idea, supported by one or more secondary ideas. To do so, sentences should employ a primary, or main, verb and as many secondary verbs as are necessary.

Third, a sentence needs a clear subject/verb structure so the reader is never confused about who or what is doing the action of the verb or verbs. To achieve these goals, a writer should follow a few basic guidelines when constructing sentences:

Writing Effective Sentences

Avoid using **it** and **there** subjects.

Keep sentences short for clarity and emphasis.

Use dependent clauses to present secondary ideas.

Use verbal phrases to present secondary ideas.

Use punctuation effectively to create clarity and emphasis.

The writer who adds these sentence-structure skills to the vocabulary and verb skills already discussed will develop the crisp, clear style necessary in any writing situation, but especially desired in the business setting.

Avoiding *It* and *There* Subjects

Although the word *it* can serve as a pronoun, too often writers use the expletives *it* and *there* as the subjects of their sentences. Neither word conveys meaning, so to use either as a subject means, in essence, reducing the impact of the second most important word in a sentence. The most important word is the verb of that subject, but if the subject is meaningless, the effect of the verb attached to it is weakened. Sentences need a clear *who did what* focus in their subject/verb structures. *It* and *there* subjects weaken this focus and thus interfere with the reader's ability to understand a writer's point.

Let's look at an example that illustrates:

Weak

There is no prior knowledge required for this job, other than a general understanding of accounting principles.

Revised

This job requires only a general understanding of accounting principles.

The shortness of the revised sentence signals that the revision is proper. Notice also how the weak sentence uses *is*, a linking verb, as its main verb. Sentences with *it* and *there* subjects often have linking verbs as main verbs. The revised sentence uses the verb *requires* as its main verb. It also places the information in the sentence in a much clearer order by having *job requires . . . understanding*, rather than *required . . . job . . . understanding*. A second example will illustrate again the benefit we gain by avoiding the expletive subject:

Weak

It is a discussion that will be led by members of our Tax Department.

Revised

Members of our Tax Department will lead the discussion.

Again, the brevity and directness of the revised sentence indicates how much better it is than the weak one using the *it* subject. A writer who revises just to change the subject of the sentence may not notice what also happens with the verbs. The revision, however, removes the main verb *is* and substitutes for it the verb *will lead*, which was a secondary verb in the weak sentence. The revised sentence also puts the verb *will lead* in the active voice, eliminating the passive voice *will be led*, which it had in the weak sentence. Both examples illustrate the direct relationship between strong verbs and clear sentence structures. Throughout this chapter, we will see this relationship evolve.

One of the particularly gratifying aspects of revising *it* and *there* subjects is how quickly we can identify sentences that need revision. We can simply look at whether a sentence uses such a subject and by looking realize that a revision is in order. Not all sentence-structure flaws are so easy to detect!

Writing Short Sentences for Emphasis and Clarity

Recent studies in language and comprehension prove that short sentences create emphasis and clarity. Emphasis and clarity enhance a reader's ability to understand what a writer is saying. Thus, we can conclude that short sentences are an asset. This principle is somewhat general. It cannot, as with *it* and *there* subjects, be reduced to one simple revision procedure. Perhaps a series of examples will allow us to see the extent to which short sentences improve our writing. The following example shows how to edit a long, somewhat rambling, sentence:

Weak

We have scheduled the in-house Tax PD course for Thursday, September 19, and it will begin at 8 a.m. in our basement conference room and will run until 5 p.m.

Revised

The in-house Tax PD course is scheduled from 8 a.m. to 5 p.m. on Thursday, September 19. It will meet in our basement conference room.

The weak sentence attempts to provide too much information at once. The reader becomes so overloaded with *when, where, what* ideas that some of the information may not register. When the sentence is broken up so the date and time appear in one sentence and the location in a second, the ideas will be clearer for the reader. Also, the revised material is grammatically less complicated, which allows for more direct emphasis on the three points the writer is making. The weak sentence is grammatically complicated because it has two compound structures joined by *and*, a compound sentence created by two independent clauses, and the compound verb *will begin . . . and . . . will run*. The revision has neither compound structure and relies only on two simple sentences to convey the same number of ideas.

We should further consider this matter of complicated grammatical structure. Such structures often result in a stilted syntax, or word order, that hides from our readers those points needing emphasis. Let's look at another example, this time one with an important idea buried in a *hidden* clause:

Weak

This new procedure for determining deductible business expenses, **which is in accord with IRS guidelines,** will save our corporate clients as much as 10 percent on their taxes.

Revised

The new, **IRS-approved** procedure for determining deductible business expenses will save our corporate clients as much as 10 percent on their taxes.

By simply taking the idea from the internal dependent clause—*which is in accord with IRS guidelines*—and presenting it in a modifier—*IRS-approved*—we have significantly shortened the sentence and lessened its grammatical complexity. The reader gets the necessary information without the risk of missing the point buried in the *hidden* clause in the weak sentence.

Sometimes modifiers add to a sentence's length and cause us to extend sentences unnecessarily. Consider the following example:

Weak

This ad would be more striking if the **background was red in color.**

Revised

This ad would be more striking with a **red background.**

This seemingly simple revision to avoid redundancy actually adds considerably to the clarity of the sentence. Sometimes the simplest revisions can make the greatest difference, and the shorter a sentence is, the more it can say to a reader.

Dependent Clauses

Short sentences are a definite asset in our writing. However, the excessive use of short sentences can have two drawbacks. It can lead to a choppy prose style, and it can lead to a writer's separating related ideas. Yet, to be sure that sentences state only one primary idea, we often find ourselves writing prose characterized by both problems. By using dependent clauses effectively, we can avoid this choppy style, keep related ideas together in the same sentence, *and* limit our sentences to one primary idea.

Let's begin with a working definition of dependent clause. A dependent clause has a subject and verb, as does an independent clause. However, the subject/verb structure in a dependent clause is subordinated by a conjunction. For example, *the report was late* is an independent clause with a subject, *report*, and verb, *was*. If we place the subordinating conjunction *because* in front of this clause—*because the report was late*—we have a dependent clause. The verb in the dependent clause is a secondary verb. It does not refer to a primary action or condition. Therefore, when we use sentences with dependent clauses, we have not presented more than one primary idea. Let's pursue this notion by looking at an example:

Weak

The report was late. We decided to reschedule the meeting.

Revised

Because the report was late, we decided to reschedule the meeting.

This example illustrates what can happen when we attempt to write short sentences. In the weak example, the style is too choppy, and two related ideas—related by cause and effect—are awkwardly separated. If, however, we place the first sentence in a dependent clause and attach it to the second, we have a stronger sentence. This revised sentence presents the intended idea much more clearly and does so in a manner that lets the reader recognize the cause-and-effect relationship between the report's being late and the decision to reschedule the meeting. The relationship between the two was implied in the first example but is directly established in the second. We see, therefore, that the effective use of dependent clauses can considerably enhance our ability to write clear sentences connecting related ideas while keeping the idea stated in the independent clause the only primary idea in the sentence.

The one danger with using dependent clauses is that we will place what should be the primary verb in a sentence in the dependent, not the independent clause. Let's look at a previously used example to illustrate:

Weak

It is a discussion that **will be led** by members of our Tax Department.

Revised

Members of our Tax Department **will lead** the discussion.

When we originally discussed this sentence, we examined the problem of the *it* subject. The sentence has a further problem, however. The main verb in the sentence is *is;* however, the primary action to which the sentence refers is *led*. In the weak sentence this action appears in passive voice and in the verb of the dependent, not the independent, clause. Thus, the impact of this verb, and therefore the idea it conveys, is reduced, both in the sentence and in the reader's mind. The revised sentence not only removes the *it* subject and substitutes the active voice *will lead* for the passive voice *will be led*, but also it places the verb conveying the primary action in the independent clause. These three benefits are related, but for us to improve our writing skills, we need to see all three benefits resulting from the revision.

Now, let's look at a second example:

Weak

Jones **found** three errors in the Abrams, Inc., audit, which **caused** the head of the Tax Department **to order** a review of all the audits performed since the new IRS changes.

Revised

After Jones **found** three errors in the Abrams, Inc., audit, the head of the Tax Department **ordered** a review of all the audits performed since the new IRS changes.

The weak sentence places little emphasis on the primary action, the head's decision *to order* new audits. This verb appears not only in the dependent clause in the weak sentence but in an infinitive as well. The verbs *found* and *caused* receive greater emphasis as a result. The revised sentence shifts this relationship so *found* is the verb of the dependent clause, and *ordered* becomes the verb of the independent clause. With this shift in sentence structure and a corresponding shift in emphasis, the writer better captures the appropriate relationship between the primary and secondary verbs.

Verbal Phrases

A second tool for enhancing a sentence by adding a secondary verb is the use of the verbal phrase. As when using a dependent clause, a writer can employ a verbal phrase to add to a sentence a second verb, or action, without obscuring the primary idea in the sentence. Often, in fact, the verbal phrase is more effective and more efficient than the dependent clause in enhancing a sentence's meaning.

The most effective verbal phrases are the participle and gerund. A participle is an *-ing* or *-ed* ending verb used as a modifier. A gerund is an *-ing* ending verb used as a noun. The following sentence presents two examples of the participle:

Arriving at the meeting several minutes early, Jones found several **infuriated** employees who had been blocked from attending ready to protest on the streets.

The sentence is filled with verbs, but most are verbal phrases. *Arriving* and *infuriated* are participles. The sentence still has only one main point, *Jones found employees*, but that central point is significantly enhanced by the use of the other verbs. In fact, these verbs create a strong, almost visual, image for the reader. Notice what happens to this sentence when all the secondary verbs are switched to appear in dependent clauses:

When **Jones arrived** at the meeting several minutes early, **he found** that several **employees who were blocked** from attending **were** infuriated and ready to protest in the streets.

While not a particularly weak sentence, this revision does not have the same directness as the one that relies on verbals; it has too many subject/verb structures: *Jones arrived, he found, employees were*, and *who were blocked*. The previous sentence managed to state all the same actions without relying so heavily on these subject/verb combinations. Such simplicity makes the verbal phrase an ideal tool for the writer who wishes to produce efficient and focused sentences. Let's consider an example illustrating the effective use of a gerund:

Weak

After **he had examined** the proposed maintenance schedule for the new equipment, the supervisor suggested several changes.

Revised

After **examining** the proposed maintenance schedule for the new equipment, the supervisor suggested several changes.

The revised sentence takes the introductory dependent clause of the weak sentence—*After he had examined the proposed maintenance schedule for the new equipment*—and by using a gerund, *examining*, converts it to a prepositional phrase. As a result, the revised sentence has one, not two, subject/verb structures, or clauses. This revision leads to a somewhat less-complicated grammatical structure and thus a more direct relationship between the two actions in the sentence, *examining* and *suggested*.

To suggest that all dependent clauses be rewritten to create verbal phrases would be poor advice. Both clauses and phrases enhance our prose by allowing us to keep one primary idea in a sentence while adding related, secondary ideas. Both allow the writer to overcome the choppy style that results from an excessive use of one-clause sentences. The verbal phrase, like the dependent clause, is thus merely a tool used to achieve an end, not the end itself. Our goal must be to understand all the tools available to us so we can use them to create emphasis, variety, and balance in our writing.

Punctuating for Emphasis

Sentence structure and punctuation are parallel concerns. The way we structure sentences determines the way we punctuate them. However, punctuation can also be a tool for giving our sentences the impact we want. And while a complete review of punctuation rules is beyond the scope of our primary concern with sentence structure, we can profit by looking specifically at how the dash, semicolon, and colon can create particular emphasis in our sentences.

The dash, semicolon, and colon call for a greater pause than does the comma. This extra pause allows a writer to join two ideas in a sentence in such a way as to stress the idea following the punctuation. Such additional emphasis may be just what a writer wants.

Let's begin by examining a basic compound sentence:

The company will conduct a national search for a statistician, for we must find someone with the skill to resolve our quality-control problems.

This sentence makes two statements; however, the second one clearly indicates the primary concern. The need for a skilled statistician has dictated the scope of the search. As structured, however, this sentence does not grammatically indicate the primacy of the second statement. We might edit in several ways to indicate more effectively the significance of the second idea, the company's need for a highly skilled employee. The best solution is to use a semicolon to create a significant pause in the sentence while still connecting related ideas:

The company will conduct a national search for a statistician; we must find someone with the skill to solve our quality-control problems.

The greater pause caused by the semicolon creates a sense of anticipation in the reader; it heightens the reader's attention to the statement that will follow. This anticipation and attention cause the reader to react with intensified interest to the second statement in the sentence, creating the emphasis the writer wants. The semicolon has this desired effect in a sentence with two independent clauses. A dash will have the same effect in a sentence that does not use two independent clauses. Sometimes a writer wishes not to use an independent clause to convey an idea. That idea might appear in a phrase or even a single word following an independent clause. The idea following the independent clause may, however, need emphasis and may even be the primary point in the sentence. Clearly such a situation is an exception to most of the stylistic and rhetorical concepts we have thus far discussed. But the point is valid, nonetheless. Let's consider an example.

The company policy on unapproved software is perfectly clear. We are not to use it.

By combining these two sentences and using a dash to separate the primary point, that the policy is not to use unapproved software, we can create particular emphasis for the main idea:

The company policy on unapproved software is perfectly clear—don't use it.

Joining the two ideas in one sentence, adding a pause to build expectation, then shortening the second idea to an almost clipped statement creates special emphasis for the three words that state the company policy. The employee who reads this statement should clearly understand what action is unacceptable. In such cases, the dash, like the semicolon, proves to be an extremely effective tool for creating sentence structures with emphasis.

The previous example uses a dash to separate ideas in a single sentence in order to stress the second point. A colon could serve the same purpose. The colon has a specific use in such situations. When the second of the two ideas explains or elaborates on the first, the colon is correct punctuation between the two. In fact, since in the previous example the first idea refers to the company policy, and the second idea states that policy, the writer would have been correct to use the colon to provide the following sentence:

The company policy on unapproved software is perfectly clear: Don't use it.

Here we see that the writer has two tools to serve essentially the same purpose, the dash and the colon. Which to use is as much a matter of individual choice as it is rule of grammar. In either case, a writer should realize that such use of punctuation to create emphasis becomes less effective the more it is used and should, therefore, make sound judgments about when to use punctuation for this effect.

Summary

We have been concerned in this chapter with techniques for producing direct, efficient prose. We began with a general rule for what we should not do:

Avoid using **it** and **there** subjects.

We then examined a series of principles about what we should do:

Use short sentences for emphasis.

Use dependent clauses and verbal phrases for combining related ideas in one sentence.

Use punctuation to create emphasis.

The writer who can balance all these techniques will have the ability to write prose characterized by sentences that are both direct and varied. Combined with the vocabulary skills already discussed, these sentence-structure skills will establish a firm foundation for writing effective memos, letters, and reports.

Exercises

I.   **Avoiding *It* and *There* Subjects:**   Rewrite the following sentences to remove all *it* and *there* subjects.

1.   There have been several occasions recently when the CEO has openly disagreed with the board of directors.

2.   It seems the board is ready to remove him as a result.

3.   I need to know when it will be possible for us to continue with the design project.

4.   The foreman asked me if there is some way we could bypass the fused circuits on the discharger.

5.   It is not difficult to compute the margin of error on a stratified survey.

6.   Check to see if there have been any complaints received by the company about the design of the X-10.

7.   There were several suggestions made by the designer about improving that model.

8.   It will take about two weeks to check all our programs for a virus.

9.   It has been suggested by some analysts that the market will peak before the end of the third quarter.

10.   There will be at least three announcements to appear in next week's newsletter about the negotiations.

II.   **Revising for Emphasis, Clarity, and Variety:**   Revise the following sentences and sentence combinations to enhance their clarity and emphasis. For variety, use any of the following techniques: shorter sentences, dependent clauses, verbal phrases, or punctuation. In each case, you should decide which technique will create the best revision.

1.   Several of Frotray's directors, primarily those who have been most recently appointed, expressed a serious concern about a recent problem, and that was the number of sexual harassment complaints filed against senior officers.

2.   After Mr. Johnston had completed his analysis of our quality-control measures, he prepared a proposal for the board in which he recommended seven remedial measures.

3.   Health-care reform may threaten pharmaceutical company profits. We will not encourage investments in these companies for the next six months.

4.   The planning and design tasks that are Ms. Levis' current responsibility involve more management skills than have been demonstrated in the jobs of the other two candidates.

5.   The company has experienced a serious retention problem with its employees for the last three years, and that problem has led to a serious increase in training costs of more than 50 percent during the same period.

6. The human resource director's statement was perfectly clear about employees' punching the time clock for each other, and that statement was that no employee is to log another employee in or out.

7. The new benefits package, the one the union had negotiated, was considered by most members to have caved in on most of the crucial demands.

8. After the committee voted to alter the research and development budget, the CEO, who had been pushing an increase for several months and who had lobbied the members of the committee individually, announced, to everyone's surprise, that he had heard from several board members that they were not going to approve the increase.

9. The new extension rods, which are made of stainless steel and are 34 cm. longer than those previously used, will be available within the month.

10. The Chamber of Commerce has promoted education reform for more than two years, but now that such reform appears to be possible, several members of the Chamber have begun to question the increase in taxes that will be necessary to fund that reform.

III. **Paragraph Editing:** Revise the following paragraph according to the advice on sentence structure presented in this chapter. Many of the decisions you make will be based on your judgment, so be sure you have a reason before making a change.

The new line supervisor in the Frame Division has submitted a report in which he has outlined several problems that he feels are responsible for the low production that has been plaguing that division. The first problem that he identifies is that employees are working with equipment that they have not been specifically trained to use. There are often significant differences that he has identified between the preparation workers have and the actual tasks that they are expected to perform, and he feels that this is the primary reason for poor productivity. His report also indicates that absenteeism in the Frame Division is 15 percent higher than that which is experienced by the plant as a whole. It is also noted in his report that he can find no reason for the higher absenteeism, but that he is willing to speculate that there is a relationship between the poor training and a low morale that can cause employees to be absent from work. The third problem in the department noted in the supervisor's report is that because the Frame Division operates some of the company's oldest equipment, down time and a lack of spare parts leave many workers idle for what he calls "extended periods." These three problems, taken together, the line supervisor speculates, could be the causes for low productivity, and he adds that until the division has newer equipment and better training for its workers, productivity will continue to be low.

IV. **Writing and Editing Your Own Work:**   For this exercise you might use a previously written paper or write an extended paragraph on one of the following topics: an assessment of your writing skills, your current graduation status, the most effective advertisement you have seen recently, your reaction to recent trends in the way the media cover news stories. Read your paragraph carefully, looking for problems with *it* or *there* subjects, sentences you can shorten to create emphasis or clarity, sentences that can be rewritten to use dependent clauses or verbals effectively, and opportunities for altered sentence structure or punctuation to create emphasis.

Writing for a Specific Reader and Purpose

Overview

*T*he first three chapters of this textbook have discussed the vocabulary and sentence-structure skills a writer should command. Generally, these principles of effective writing apply regardless of the situation or the reader. Sometimes to make a memo, letter, or report work, however, we have to consider more than general principles of style. We must also consider our purpose and audience. For example, we do not want to waste our readers' time telling them what they already know. We do not want to alienate our readers with an improper tone caused by careless word choice and sentence structure or offend them with language that raises the issue of gender in what should be a gender-neutral situation. We should always select language that moves our readers to act in accord with our purpose for writing in the first place. In short, after writers have mastered language and sentence-structure skills, they adapt their work based on how they answer the following questions:

Writing for Purpose and Reader

Is the primary purpose to inform or persuade the reader?

Should the tone be authoritative, cooperative, or objective?

Is the language gender-neutral?

Audience and Purpose

Much of what makes an effective writer follows from common sense, and nowhere does common sense become more of a factor in our writing than in deciding exactly what we need to say to a reader. Let's look at the following memo and use common sense to decide what the writer could have omitted to reach the point more directly:

MEMORANDUM

TO: Jane Franks, Division Supervisor

FROM: Bill Wilson, Laboratory Supervisor

DATE: January 14, 1996

RE: Missing DX-2

During a **routine inventory** conducted on January 13, 1996, it was discovered that 43 grams of DX-2 are missing from the chemical supply room. **Inventories are conducted on a regular basis at the end of each month;** therefore, it can be assumed that the chemical has been missing for at most four weeks. **As you know, this chemical is strictly regulated by the FDA because of its utilization in the manufacture of several illegal drugs.** A review of the supply-room log provided no indication of when or by whom the chemical was taken. **All chemists in my laboratory have keys to the supply room as per company policy,** but they are to leave log entries whenever they take supplies. **A full investigation shall be initiated, and your advice will be most appreciated.**

You may have already noticed several matters of style that need attention. For the moment, let's put those aside and consider instead how poorly this memo responds to the writer's purpose and audience. First, a division supervisor already would be aware of matters of company policy and needs no reminder that all the chemists have keys. Second, this reader is aware of FDA regulations; the writer even says *As you know.* Third, we might note that inventories are described as *regular, routine,* and *conducted at the end of each month.* The reader does not need quite this many statements indicating that things have been handled properly. Finally, the last sentence seems to address two purposes. Is the writer sending information? or seeking help? A rewritten version of this memo offers a more appropriate handling of audience and purpose:

MEMORANDUM

TO: Jane Franks, Division Supervisor

FROM: Bill Wilson, Laboratory Supervisor   *BW*

DATE: January 14, 1996

RE: Missing DX-2

During a routine inventory on January 13, 1996, **it was discovered** that 43 grams of DX-2 are missing from the chemical supply room. Inventories **are conducted** monthly; therefore, **it can be assumed** that the chemical has been missing for at most four weeks. A review of the supply-room log, which chemists sign when taking supplies, provided no **indication** of when or by whom the chemical was taken. A full **investigation shall be initiated** should you wish to offer advice.

The memo is considerably shorter once the material the reader already knows is eliminated. This version of the memo lets the writer concentrate on the more immediate concern, the missing chemical. Still, problems with style remain. In essence, what the memo needs is two levels of revision, one to deal with audience and purpose and the other to deal with word choice and sentence structure. Let's look at a revision that corrects the problems with style:

MEMORANDUM

TO: Jane Franks, Division Supervisor

FROM: Bill Wilson, Laboratory Supervisor   *BW*

DATE: January 14, 1996

RE: Missing DX-2

During a routine inventory on January 13, 1992, I discovered that 43 grams of DX-2 are missing from the chemical supply room. Because inventories are monthly, I assume that the chemical has been missing for at most four weeks. I have reviewed the supply room log, which chemists sign when taking supplies, but found no entry to indicate when or by whom the chemical was taken. I will investigate and welcome your advice.

Now the memo not only has the appropriate content for the reader and purpose it serves but also uses the strong, verb-based style that assists all readers. A feature of style resulting from the emphasis on verbs is the use of the first-person pronoun *I*. Later in this chapter, we will look at the problems that *can* result from a poor use of the first person. Here, however, the first person allows the writer to use strong verbs and to sound "in command" of his responsibilities. Given the situation, this writer should be and sound in control, so the style is appropriate to this objective.

Let's look at another example of careless writing that takes into account neither the needs of a reader nor the purpose of the writer. The following is an entry in a shift log used in a manufacturing setting to monitor basic activities:

Shift 3 LOG: September 4, 1996, 4:34 a.m.

It was observed that the inflow pressure valve for the DX-2 was reading at 867 psi. It was noted that **this reading is above the required 850 psi necessary for the flow of DX-2 to maintain itself at a safe and efficient level.** It was recorded at 4 a.m. that the psi was 853, **which is within acceptable limits.** An appropriate adjustment was made to bring the pressure back to a correct reading. According to standard company procedures, all product produced between 4 a.m. and 4:34 a.m. **must be discharged as waste.**

Anyone reading such a shift log should know basic company operations well enough to follow the writer's point without so much detail about the obvious. Again, we should note the ineffective style; as with the previous example, we will return to this sample later to correct these problems. For the moment, let's consider the purpose and audience for this entry and make content revisions to help the writer more specifically address the necessary points.

First, a shift log serves two basic purposes: It helps those workers on a subsequent shift know what has recently taken place, and it provides a permanent record of a shift's activities in the event that a later review becomes necessary. Such review of a log is common in industry after a problem occurs or a worker receives an injury when an investigator looks for the causes of that problem or injury. In both cases, the readers should already be aware of the basic safety and efficiency requirements of the process they are monitoring. What all readers *do* need, however, is to know exactly what actions were taken; the final sentence, using the verb *must be discharged*, leaves at least part of that message unclear. Does this verb signal that that action *was taken* or remains *to be taken?* A reader would assume that the writer on the previous shift would have discharged the damaged product, but the verb, because it is in passive voice, leaves the question open. Consider how much more appropriate the following log entry would be given the writer's purpose and the reader's needs:

Shift 3 LOG: September 4, 1996, 4:34 a.m.

It was observed that the inflow pressure valve for DX-2 was reading at 867 psi. **It was recorded** at 4 a.m. that the psi was 853. An appropriate **adjustment was made** to bring the pressure back to a correct reading. All product produced between 4 a.m. and 4:34 a.m. **was discharged** as waste.

Now this log entry avoids telling the reader that the 867 psi is above a safe and efficient level; the reader would know this. It also avoids the unnecessary "acceptable limits" discussion. The reader knows company procedure, and the revised entry reflects this fact. Finally, the verb *was discharged* clarifies the actions the writer took. The entry is, in short, much more appropriate for the reader and purpose. The problems with style, however, remain and need attention:

Shift 3 LOG: September 4, 1996, 4:34 a.m.

I observed that the inflow pressure valve for DX-2 was 867 psi. At 4 a.m. the reading was 853. I adjusted the pressure to bring it back to a proper level and discharged as waste all product produced between 4 a.m. and 4:34 a.m.

All this entry needs now is a signature (or initials) to identify the *I* pronoun or the writer. Otherwise, the strong verbs and edited content make this an efficient and helpful log entry. Anyone who has worked in a professional setting knows how helpful short log entries, memos, and letters can be. They allow readers to determine what they need to know and get back to their duties quickly.

If we examine our experiences revising first the DX-2 memo and then the DX-2 log entry, we can develop a system for considering how our purpose and our audience should affect the way we approach our writing. Such a strategy might be depicted as follows:

Figure 1

Purpose and Adaptation

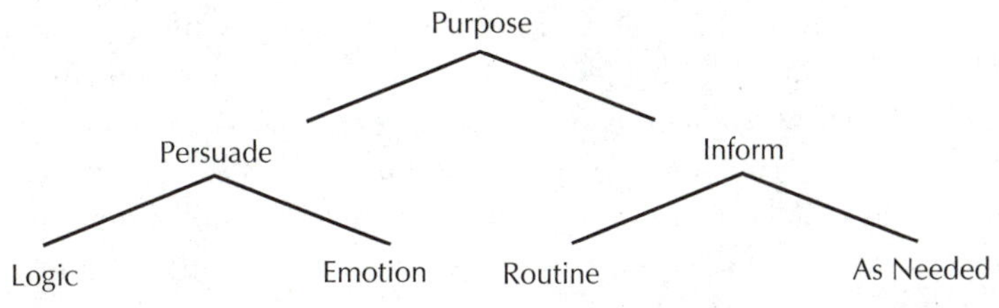

While most business documents provide information that the readers need, certainly others attempt to persuade readers to take some action or hold a certain opinion. With each document we write, therefore, we should consider first what we hope to accomplish, then adapt our material to help us fulfill that objective. Primarily our purpose will affect the *tone, organization,* or *content* of our memo, letter, or report. The needs of our readers also affect these aspects of our writing, and at times the demands of purpose and reader seem to overlap.

If our purpose is simply to inform our reader, then the tone should be objective. We make a mistake when writing a report with no persuasive purpose if we use an aggressive or even cooperative tone that seems designed to convince the reader to take some action or hold some opinion. The reader would be confused by a tone that suggests a purpose the writer did not intend.

If, on the other hand, we are attempting to persuade the reader, we should strive for either an aggressive or cooperative tone, whichever seems most likely to be effective with our reader. In this situation, the writer faces a major and often difficult decision—determining whether a given reader will be more likely to respond favorably to an aggressive or to a cooperative tone. Taking the time to consider the reader and adapt tone effectively may make the difference between a persuasive argument—one that fulfills our purpose—and one that does not work. Already we can see how purpose and reader overlap, and we will continue this discussion after completing our review of ways to adapt a document based on our purpose.

The way we organize our ideas in a document can also depend on our purpose. A basic information report will often proceed in a methodical, deductive order. This order places the context information—a discussion of the situation that has created the need for the material the document provides—first. Following will be the information itself. The document will conclude with any analysis and conclusions the reader needs to be fully informed. In a persuasive document, on the other hand, the writer may need to pull the reader in by placing important conclusions, or a summary of them, at the beginning of the document. The reader who sees such important material immediately will be more likely to comprehend the importance of the document and then read it carefully.

Content, too, is affected by our purpose. When we are providing routine information to keep a reader informed, we need less introductory material, while an *as needed* report will likely require more introductory information to set the stage for the reader. An *as needed* report deals with a situation that has arisen outside the course of normal business activity, such as a retail company's needing to deal with a road construction project that will alter its customers' access to its facilities. With such a document, the reader may be unaware of the problem that led to the study contained in the report and can best understand a writer's conclusions about how to solve the problem if introductory material provides a detailed discussion. Routine reports, however, deal with familiar situations, so the reader does not need an extensive context-setting review. Purpose also affects the writer's decision about visual content. All reports benefit from visuals. Tables tend to work well in information reports. The visual impact and drama of tables and graphs enhance a document's persuasive capacity.

In many respects, these methods of adaptation follow from simple common sense. As the discussion of tone would suggest, they also must coincide with effective audience analysis. What follows is an outline of an audience-analysis procedure:

Figure 2
Audience and Adaptation

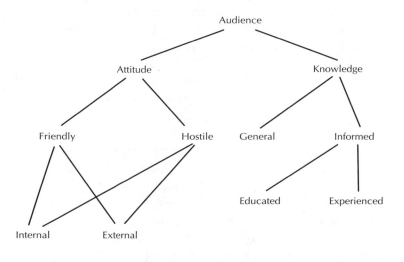

This audience-analysis diagram indicates how our readers' characteristics can influence the decisions we must make as writers. We must consider not only what they know about the material we are presenting, but also how they may feel about that material. We need to keep in mind, as well, what kind of professional relationship we have with our readers. Their knowledge will affect the content of our documents, particularly in the amount of detail we have to provide about technical material and background information. Our readers' attitudes about our material, especially in documents that provide analysis and draw conclusions, is also a serious concern. Attitude should influence our tone. Potentially hostile readers, for example, should cause a writer to maintain an objective tone, while readers who are friendly toward us and our ideas will less likely be concerned if our tone is less objective.

In both cases, documents intended for external readers—ones outside our company—should possess a more formal style and presentation than would be necessary for internal readers, ones who work where we work. This aspect of audience analysis also affects our content. In most cases, external readers would require more context detail than would internal ones. Just as we adapt a document to purpose, then, we should make careful decisions about adapting it to the needs and demands of our audience. The diagram on audience analysis presented here reflects general analyses, as did the one on purpose; we should not see either as absolute guidelines. Writers should always be sensitive to the uniqueness of any writing situation. We must consider both audience and purpose according to their demands each time we write. Before going further, let's look at one more example of adapting a document to the demands of a specific writing purpose and reader.

One common type of business letter makes an offer. The success of a company may well depend on the effectiveness of such letters. The purpose is clear—to get the reader to purchase a service or product. Often, such letters are directed at a specific category of reader, identified by careful marketing research. Others go to a more general audience, especially letters offering a service or product with potentially broad appeal. The following example is the introductory paragraph from a letter marketing a travelers' protection plan. The letter was sent to a large audience, all persons who hold gasoline-company credit cards but who have not yet joined those companies' travelers protection clubs. As you read this introductory paragraph, consider the effectiveness of the presentation. Remember that while the purpose of the entire letter will be to outline the details of membership, the particular purpose of the first paragraph is to capture the readers' interest so they will continue reading and thus learn exactly what membership entails:

Automobile Owners' Association
101 Motorist Highway
Sal Perno, California 34343

May 12, 1996

Dear Auto Owner,

Enclosed in this letter is an **offer** of membership in the Automobile Owners' Association that must receive serious **consideration. Participants** in AOA receive auto-theft insurance, 24-hour wrecker service, and many other benefits. These services mean **protection** of vacations and business trips. They may be the difference between an emergency and a minor inconvenience. For **those** who are interested, this letter provides a full **explanation** of the many reasons for joining the Automobile Owners' Association.

This paragraph is characterized by two features of language in particular. First, it maintains an extremely objective tone and thus contains no personal pronouns. Because the purpose of the letter in general, certainly the purpose of the first paragraph, is to persuade the reader that the product being offered is worth buying, a warmer, thereby more persuasive, tone would be more effective. The objective tone also results in most of the paragraph's important points appearing as nouns: *offer, consideration, Participants, protection,* and *explanation.* The absence of personal pronouns, especially the *you* pronoun, keeps the offer distant. The reader is never *pulled* into the memo. Because of the lack of action verbs, the reader never receives the message: "You should act." And action is what the writer wants! Let's look at what happens when we change just these two features of style:

Automobile Owners' Association
101 Motorist Highway
Sal Perno, California 34343

May 12, 1996

Dear Auto Owner,

This letter **offers** Automobile Owners' Association membership, which **you should seriously consider.** When **you join** AOA, **you receive** auto-theft insurance, 24-hour wrecker service, and many other benefits. These services will **protect your vacations and business trips.** They may determine whether **you suffer** an emergency or **experience** a minor inconvenience. **Interested?** This letter **explains** fully why **you will want to join** the Automobile Owners' Association.

Consider the rewritten letter in terms of the marketing concept *AIDA: Attention, Interest, Desire, Action.* The *you* pronouns get the *Attention* of the readers and pull them into the offer. The verbs create the atmosphere of *Action.* And when the two are related, as in phrases such as *you receive, will protect your,* and *you suffer . . .* or (you) *experience,* then the readers will be even more *Interested* and have a *Desire* to respond to the letter.

The attention to reader and purpose seen in this revised letter, combined with our earlier discussion of style, suggests just how much care must go into our writing. And, yet, we should also be able to see how simple common sense helps us make good decisions when we write. Common sense, for example, says use *you* pronouns to pull a reader into an offer. Common sense says use action words when trying to get a reader to act.

Most of the revisions of this paragraph were necessary to remove its cold, objective tone. Tone, however, is a complex concept and is one of the most difficult characteristics of our writing to control. Our discussion of audience and purpose would not be complete without analyzing the features of language that have the greatest impact on tone.

Using Proper Tone

Sometimes our message is correct, but the manner in which we present it is so flawed that we damage communication. Words and sentence structures can create emotion, and emotion often inhibits effective business; only in special circumstances does it contribute to efficient business or clear communication. When we write, we must, therefore, be aware of how the choice of words and the structure of our sentences can make readers react to the *how* rather than the *what* in our writing. Notice how authoritative the following memo is because of the way it is written:

MEMORANDUM

TO: All Office Personnel

FROM: Craig Sheldon, Office Manager   *CS*

DATE: January 13, 1996

RE: Use of Unauthorized Software

Recently, I walked in on a video game being played on one of our computers. What **I think each of you will comprehend,** after my having **stressed to you** the importance of **not** introducing outside software to our system, is that I was more than a little **angry.**

You seem to think that if a program is not copied to the "C" drive and is run only on the "A" drive, it will not contaminate the system with a virus. **Understand** that this is not the case.

Use any program already installed on the "C" drive, the network drive, or provided to you on floppy diskette by the company. Confidence and knowledge of computers in the work place is built through your use of these programs.

In **my opinion, any of you** who risk contaminating our system deserve **immediate dismissal.**

The issue is not whether this memo deals with a serious situation; it does. The issue is whether the tone in this memo will cause people to cooperate or whether it will discourage them from doing so. The threat of being fired may force the readers to refrain from using outside software, but what about future efforts to cooperate? Has one memo with an overly aggressive tone damaged the relationship between the writer and readers? Perhaps. With some attention to language, the writer can give the same forceful message in a form that does not alienate the readers. We can best begin to answer this question by looking specifically at features of language that contribute to the overly aggressive tone in the memo.

We should first observe the excessive use of the first person pronouns—*I* and *my*—as well as the shift from *I* to *you*. We noted earlier how the effective use of first person helps eliminate certain problems with style. In this situation, however, the use of first-person pronouns adds to the aggressive tone. Words such as *comprehend, stressed,* and *angry* in this situation enhance that tone. This memo also has two command sentences, those beginning *Understand* and *Use*. Commands are certainly aggressive. And finally, by underlining the word *not*, the writer chose to stress the negative sentence. Taken together, these decisions create an aggressive tone that might cause the readers to react to the *how* rather than the *what* in the memo. This reaction is not what the writer wants.

The problems in this memo suggest a system for working on tone. By pointing to the four features of language that most affect the emotions expressed in our writing, we can determine whether we achieve an authoritative, cooperative, or objective tone. Let's look at those four features and what conclusions we can draw from each:

Pronouns

Authoritative tone is created by the use of **I** pronouns, particularly when combined with a shift in a sentence from **I**, meaning the writer, to **you,** meaning the reader.

Cooperative tone is created by the use of **we** pronouns, when the **we** means the reader and the writer, not the writer and others with power over the reader. This second **we** is the company **we,** and it can be intimidating to a reader.

Objective tone is created either by a balance of the **I, you, we** pronouns or by the use of the third-person pronouns and nouns. **One,** for example, in place of **you** is objective, but it is also very formal.

General Word Choice

Authoritative tone is created by large, stiff-sounding words, especially those with negative connotations such as **termination** or **implementation.**

Cooperative tone is created by simpler words with no judgmental connotations such as **start** or **dismissed.**

Objective tone is created simply by using words with as few connotations as possible and according to their exact dictionary meaning.

Sentence Type

Authoritative tone is created by command structures.

Cooperative tone is created by the occasional use of the rhetorical question.

Objective tone is created by consistent use of declarative sentences that simply make a statement.

Mode

Authoritative tone is created when ideas are unnecessarily presented in negative terms.

Cooperative tone is created when ideas appear consistently in a positive mode.

Objective tone is created when the negative and positive are used according to the demands of the writer's idea, not as a means of passing judgment.

Now let's consider how the previous memo might appear if it keeps these basic rules in mind. Remember, we are not looking at the message in the memo but, rather, at how the writer conveys that message:

MEMORANDUM

TO: All Office Personnel

FROM: Craig Sheldon, Office Manager *CS*

DATE: January 13, 1996

RE: Use of Unauthorized Software

Recently, I walked in on a video game being played on one of our computers. This **concerned** me, particularly given the recent emphasis on the importance of not using outside software with the company's system. **We** all need to keep in mind that a program run on drive "A" can contaminate the system with a virus.

All of us should use the programs installed on drive "C" to improve our knowledge of and confidence with the company's computer system. **We** must, however, limit ourselves to those programs.

But I must say here that any employee who risks contaminating the system by using outside software will also risk being dismissed.

We have kept the first sentence. And the last sentence makes clear that violating this company policy could cost someone's job. To diminish this point would be unfair. But the revised final sentence is better because the words *opinion* and *immediate* are gone. Moreover, the tone throughout has become cooperative because of the shift to *we* pronouns, the omission of the commands that appear at the end of the second paragraph and the beginning of the third, the use of the positive mode in the first paragraph, and the overall *softer* word choice that results from removing *stressed, comprehend,* and *angry.* The memo no longer has a condescending, authoritative tone and will probably, as a result, generate more cooperation from the readers.

To repeat, tone is perhaps the most difficult of all aspects of our writing to control. We also have to be careful about overgeneralizing when discussing tone. At least with these basic guidelines, we have something more exact than the vague word "tone" to work with. And of course, no one tone is suited to all situations. While we have worked on softening tone, the same principles would help us move to a more aggressive tone if that is what we want. Let's consider a memo that has the elements of the cooperative tone but that might be too gentle to get some readers to react:

MEMORANDUM

TO:	Harold Johns
FROM:	Davis Wilson, Supervisor *DW)* Parts Division
DATE:	October 24, 1996
RE:	Recent Absences

I wish to express **concern** about your work during the past two weeks. The assembly foreman has twice indicated that parts you were to transport had not arrived, thus holding up his work. The result has been stalled assembly lines. **I am aware that we have had several workers absent this week, which may have contributed to this difficulty.** Whatever the case, **could you check with me so we can work things out?**

The second sentence of this memo makes clear that the reader is responsible for the problem when it says *you were to transport.* The rest of the memo, however, makes excuses for the reader, so the content backs away from that assignment of responsibility. Also, the tone is extremely gentle, so much so that the reader could be led into not taking the problem as seriously as he should. The gentle **we** contributes to this tone, as does the rhetorical question that ends the memo. The language, too, lacks an edge, as the writer chooses *to express concern*, acknowledge a *difficulty* rather than a *problem*, and *to work things out* with the person whose failures have created the situation. This memo might have exactly the approach a supervisor should take with some employees; if, however, this employee needs a stronger message, the memo might appear as follows:

MEMORANDUM

TO: Harold Johns

FROM: Davis Wilson, Supervisor *DW)*
             Parts Division

DATE: October 24, 1996

RE: Recent Absences

I write to point out to you that your work during the past two weeks has **not been acceptable.** On two occasions, the assembly foreman has **strongly complained** that parts you were to transport had not arrived, thus holding up his work. **We** cannot continue to **suffer** the cost of stalled assembly lines because of **your failure** to perform. I am aware that we've had several workers absent this week, but I **cannot accept any excuse** for this level of performance. **See me** if you have any questions.

The memo now has a strong, authoritative tone. This tone results from the shift from the cooperative *we* to the authoritative *we* and the use of sentences in which the *I* pronoun shifts to the *you* pronoun. The memo also has a negative mode with *not been acceptable* and *cannot accept.* The general word choice is also aggressive: *strongly complained, suffer, failure,* and *excuse.* Finally, the memo ends with a command. Used together, these features of language create an extremely aggressive tone.

Which of these two memos would be appropriate would depend on the employee the supervisor was dealing with. For some, the cooperative tone of the first would be most likely to produce results. Some might need the stronger second memo. If supervisors know their employees, they know which to send. With careful attention to language, they can make that knowledge of their employees and their skill as writers work together.

Sexist Language

Our concern in this chapter with correctly adapting our writing to the needs and feelings of our audience suggests that we should also concern ourselves with language that improperly reflects gender. None of us would tolerate language that even suggests religious or racial stereotyping. We are, however, perhaps less likely to detect and revise language that distinguishes gender in situations that for moral or legal reasons should be gender-neutral. Consider the following sentence:

Anyone who wants to be considered for promotion to Technician III should submit a copy of **his** last two performance ratings.

Although the sentence begins with the indefinite pronoun *Anyone*, the word *his* that later appears implies that only a male will actually receive the promotion. Traditionally, writers have used the masculine gender pronouns to refer to all people in a generic sense. The workplace has changed, however. In fact, more women than men will be entering the professions through the rest of the twentieth century. This changing nature of the professions makes clear that "traditional" usage is no longer appropriate, if it ever was.

In addition to the moral issues raised by the use of gender-specific language, such as the *his* in the example sentence, we also must consider the legal situation. Hirings and promotions cannot be based on gender; the example sentence, by merely suggesting that a promotion may be tied to gender, is inappropriate. Consider how the following revisions of the example are just as clear but more appropriate, given the situation:

Plural

Employees who want to be considered for promotion to Technician III should submit **their** last two performance ratings.

Passive Voice

The last two performance ratings **should be submitted** by anyone seeking promotion to Technician III.

Normally, we would consider passive voice a weakness. With this revision, however, it gives us a shorter, gender-neutral sentence than the active voice revision. Also effective is the shift to the plural construction demonstrated here.

Pronouns may be the most obvious part of speech to indicate gender or to stereotype based on gender. Other language, however, can also indicate gender bias. Consider the following types of language bias, using *man* and stereotyping by gender:

Weak

Conrad Corporation is seeking a **chairman** for its board of directors.

Only when we have an applicant with extensive data management experience will we have the **man** we're looking for.

Revised

Conrad Corporation is seeking a **chair** for its board of directors.

Only when we have an applicant with extensive data management experience will we have the **employee** we're looking for.

Both revisions are simple, but both avoid the implication that the companies are interested only in a male to fill positions for which women *should* be equally viable candidates.

Weak

Unfortunately, many chief executives become so preoccupied with their companies that they ignore their **wives** and children.

Any nurse who wants to work with a surgical team must have, according to hospital policy, a blood test before **she** will be approved for such duty.

Revised

Unfortunately, many chief executives become so preoccupied with their companies that they ignore their **spouses** and children.

Any nurse who wants to work with a surgical team must have, according to hospital policy, a blood test before being approved for such duty.

The revision of the first sentence is simple; the writer has the gender neutral *spouses* available to make the necessary change. The revision of the second sentence is a bit different, because the writer simply removed the pronoun *she* that created the gender stereotype. Both indicate, however, the importance of not creating gender distinctions when referring to professional positions held by both men and women. Examples of another language bias, lack of parallel treatment, and again of the use of masculine pronouns, follow:

Weak

President Bush: "I have spoken this morning with **President Mitterand, Chancellor Kohl,** and **Margaret Thatcher** about the events in the Persian Gulf."

Revised

President Bush: "I have spoken this morning with President Mitterand, Chancellor Kohl, and **Prime Minister** Thatcher about the events in the Persian Gulf."

We might question whether President Bush intended, even unconsciously, to place Minister Thatcher in a less-distinguished position than that of her male counterparts. Nonetheless, she was no less a head of state than were the men and deserved, when referred to in such an *equal* situation, to receive *equal* treatment.

Weak

I will give extra credit to anyone who gives me a rough draft of **his** paper.

Revised

I will give extra credit to students who give me a rough draft of **their** papers.

This example is identical to the one we previously examined. The revision simply demonstrates how using the plural *students . . . their* allows the writer to maintain gender neutrality.

All these examples show inappropriate gender distinctions and suggest ways to avoid them. We do not, of course, have to move to the point of using the term *personhole cover* in order to use language appropriately; we do need, however, to be aware of language that creates gender distinctions when such distinctions would be unprofessional or illegal.

Summary

The first three chapters of this text examined principles of writing that always apply because they enhance our directness and clarity. In this chapter we have looked at the importance of adapting our writing to the needs of a situation, or *purpose*, and to our *audience*. We have been particularly attentive to the issues of emotion, controlling the *tone* in our writing, and avoiding *gender-specific* language. Writers who combine the basic principles of the first four chapters and develop their writing strategy based on those principles will have the solid foundation for building effective memos, letters, and reports.

Exercises

I.   **Adapting to Audience and Purpose:**   The following paragraph comes from a technical report concerning a company's efforts to comply with EPA standards. Edit the paragraph so it addresses the needs of purpose and audience. The purpose of the report is to give information. The audience is company management, people who are well-informed about such matters as EPA standards and policies, especially as they affect the company.

The new EPA standard requires chemical companies and industries using chemical processes to control liquid and gas HCL emissions. Specifically, the EPA, which is the primary environmental agency for the federal government, demands that liquids discharged into surface or ground water contain no more HCL than 1 part per thousand; we are currently discharging liquid waste from our plastics treatment process that contains 12 parts per thousand. We are, therefore, not complying with EPA requirements. Moreover, the EPA requires that no gas emissions contain more than 3 parts per thousand HCL. Our current treatment devices only reduce HCL emissions to a level of 21 parts per thousand. Again, we do not meet EPA standards. Finally, the EPA will begin inspecting suspect facilities in January 1997. Company policy has always been to comply with EPA requirements at least one year prior to investigation. And the necessary filtering devices to conform to EPA standards are available. We could install them by January 1996. These devices, however, are extremely expensive; therefore, I recommend that we suspend company policy, maintain our current emission levels, and avoid this expense.

II. **Adapting to Audience and Purpose:** The following memo is designed to generate employee interest in a company physical-conditioning program. Edit the memo to make it more effective in attracting the interest of the employees.

MEMORANDUM

TO: All Company Employees

FROM: Jan Stevens, Human Resources Director

DATE: June 4, 1996

RE: Physical Conditioning Program

ACE, Inc., has recently built a physical conditioning facility in Plant A, which is available for employees during evenings (7-9 p.m.) and on Saturdays (9 a.m.-4 p.m.). Any employee who wishes to use the facility is encouraged to do so. Studies give the indication that people who exercise three or four times a week for a minimum of 30 minutes experience health benefits. Such exercise programs may determine whether one misses work with an illness or even enjoys a savings of money on unnecessary visits to a physician. Such savings may help the company enjoy a reduction in health-benefits coverage. Although it is not a requirement that employees use this facility, this is a free program, which would not be the case if one were to go to a health club.

III. **Adapting Tone:** The following paragraph has problems with an overly aggressive tone. Edit the memo so it has a more cooperative tone.

MEMORANDUM

TO: All Personnel

FROM: John Davis, Human Resources Director   *JD*

DATE: November 3, 1996

RE: Benefits Package Payments

Traditionally, you at ACME, Inc., have enjoyed a benefits package that goes beyond the basic requirements of the ALD Union to which most of you belong. Unfortunately, I find the company situation a bit precarious in its ability to pay for that package, and an adjustment is necessary to compensate for the shrinking flexibility with personnel costs.

Therefore, my firm decision is to not renegotiate the benefits in the package but, rather, to increase the necessary deduction from your paychecks so you absorb a greater share of the cost of the current benefits. I calculate that the change will cost you approximately $100 more per year. I have no choice but to take this action, given the current problems in the health-care industry that are driving up the costs the company incurs. But let me remind you that I have not violated the union position on this matter.

Plan your family budget to accommodate this new strain on your income because this decision will stand. I suggest that you take some comfort in the fact that for several years you have enjoyed benefits that exceed what your union considers fair.

IV. **Sexist Language:** Rewrite the following sentences to remove gender-specific language.

1. Any of my employees would be a good man for the promotion to Technician II.

2. Any employee who wants his benefits reviewed to take advantage of new tax laws should see the personnel director.

3. Although any member of my unit is trained for a dangerous assignment, such as cleaning this chemical spill, I don't want those with wives and children to provide for sent.

4. The faculty who attended the meeting were Professor David Jones, Professor Leonard Speck, and Mrs. Wilson.

5. We will need to hire a foreman with shoulders broad enough to handle the problems in the assembly plant.

6. We should include a list of duties in our ad so when a candidate applies he can indicate the specific areas in which he already has the experience we want.

7. Let's try to find out who submitted the work order late and make sure she and the other secretaries understand how important this type of mistake is.

8. I know we are involved in all fifty states, but perhaps if we send letters to all the U.S. congressmen who represent districts in which we have facilities, we can block the proposed bill to change environmental standards.

V. **Developing Tone:** The following case sets up a situation to which you will respond by letter. Write one version of the letter using an authoritative or aggressive tone and a second version with a cooperative tone. Be careful as you write that both letters say the same thing and that tone is the product of *how* you write, not *what* you write.

On October 23 of this year, you took your VCR to the local repair shop, Electronics Incorporated, to be serviced. You identified the problem for the person at the counter. Specifically, you indicated that the VCR would suddenly shut off when playing a tape. You were told that as soon as a technician examined the VCR, you would receive an estimate of cost before the work was done. Later that day, you received a call from the technician and were told that repairs would be $45. You asked the technician to proceed. On October 25, you picked up your VCR and paid the $45. That very day, when playing a tape, you found that the problem had not been fixed. You took it back to Electronics Incorporated. This time the estimate was $85, and, again, you said you wanted the work done. When you picked up the VCR, you paid the bill and left. Later, you noticed that you had been charged $20 for general servicing. You had paid $20 for general servicing in the original $45. When you called Electronics Incorporated, you were told that after any repairs, a VCR needed this work and that both $20 charges were proper. Your point was that you would not have needed the second repair work had it been done correctly the first time. You made no progress by phone, so you decided to appeal in writing to Mr. Harold Davis, Manager, Electronics Incorporated, P.O. Box 3344, Madison, NE 34343.

CHAPTER V

Effective Paragraph Organization

Overview

*J*ust as sentences are ineffective when they are constructed loosely, so, too, are paragraphs weakened by a lack of focus. Without sentence focus, the reader experiences related ideas in an order that obscures their relationships. These relationships among ideas are vital to our reader's ability to comprehend our thoughts. When paragraph structure confuses those relationships, our ability to convey our message suffers. Three basic principles of paragraph development that generally apply do, however, give us a system for keeping the relationships among ideas clear:

Writing Effective Paragraphs

Paragraphs should generally begin with a topic sentence that anticipates, and prepares the reader for, the ideas to follow.

Sentences in a paragraph should follow a logical order as the paragraph progresses.

Sentences in a paragraph should be tied together through repetition of key words, clear pronoun reference, and transition.

The value of these general principles of paragraph structure will become more apparent as we investigate each and look at examples.

Topic Sentences

With the exception of short transition paragraphs or those that simply give a summary at the end of a letter or memo, all paragraphs develop ideas. Any paragraph that develops an idea should begin with a sentence that indicates to the reader what to expect. Business writing is like all other types of writing in this respect, but we can look at examples from specific types of business documents to see just how important topic sentences can be. Consider, for example, the following sentence from the opening paragraph in a job-application letter:

I am interested in the position of Office Manager, which your firm advertised in the June 14, 1993, edition of *The Business Monitor.*

This statement fails as a topic sentence; thus, an important letter begins poorly. This sentence does not clearly indicate the writer's purpose. The writer could be sending a letter requesting more information about the position, soliciting an ad for the position to be run in another publication, or applying for the position. All three of the following topic sentences would be more effective:

I write to apply for the position of Office Manager, which your firm advertised in the June 14, 1993, edition of *The Business Monitor.*

or

I write to ask if you would be interested in listing your position of Office Manager, presented in the June 14, 1993, edition of *The Business Monitor,* in the publication *Employment Daily.*

or

I am interested in the position of Office Manager your firm advertised in the June 14, 1993, edition of *The Business Monitor* but would like additional information.

The weak topic sentence we first looked at could begin the introductory paragraph of a letter pursuing one of the purposes suggested by these three topic sentences. These would, therefore, be more appropriate options.

The most important thing to remember about a topic sentence is that its purpose is not to develop an idea, or even to begin development. Rather, it should identify for the reader what idea the writer intends to develop. Topic sentences are, in other words, structural sentences written to guide a reader by introducing what is to follow.

Paragraph Order

The most effective order for sentences to follow in a paragraph is determined by the ideas they communicate, the relationship among those ideas, and the effect the writer wishes to produce. For example, a paragraph that deals with cause-and-effect relationships will arrange sentences in an order that clearly establishes which sentences present the causes and which the effects. An appropriate order would be statements of cause preceding statements of effect. Furthermore, paragraphs dealing with the chronology of events will order statements of events according to the time those events took place.

Concern for a reader's reaction to a message might also dictate the order a paragraph presents ideas. A paragraph in a letter that presents readers with a decision they will not like would probably first state the reasons for that decision before presenting the bad news. On the other hand, a writer presenting a positive decision might prefer to open with the good news. In essence, a writer should arrange sentences in a paragraph after appropriate consideration of the ideas they convey or the impact the message could have on the reader. These two systems of order are called *deductive* and *inductive*. A paragraph written in deductive order will begin with general statements and proceed to more specific statements. A paragraph written in inductive order will begin with specific statements and proceed to more general ones.

Perhaps the most common arrangement of ideas in a paragraph is deductive, one that begins with general statements and then proceeds to more specific ones. In such a paragraph, however, the writer wants to be sure to maintain this pattern of organization. Let's look at a paragraph that does not move effectively from general to specific statements. The paragraph begins with a general statement, moves to a more specific one, broadens again to a very general assertion, and then becomes more specific at the end. The spacing of the sentences on the page will illustrate the move from general to specific statements:

ALFCO management, on the advice of the board of
directors, has increased the cost of the
health-care benefits package.

This change will result in an additional deduction of $10 per month from each
employee's paycheck.

The health-care benefits in the
package will remain the
same.

ALFCO management is concerned about its employees and
wants to do all that is possible to help them in
the area of health care.

This change would not be made were it
not necessary.

The additional deduction will
allow us to keep the
same benefits.

If you have any ques-
tions, please call
me.

One result of the confused order of this paragraph is that the writer says twice that benefits will remain the same despite the increased deduction. A desire to repeat an important idea, especially one containing good news, is natural. When the paragraph again becomes general, the writer who feels the need to focus on the good news will, therefore, do it twice. When we edit the paragraph to keep a steady movement from general to specific, however, the need to repeat this idea disappears:

ALFCO management is concerned about its employees and
wants to do all that is possible to help them
in the area of health care.

On the advice of the board of directors, however, management has increased the cost
of its health-care benefits package.

This change would not be made were it not
necessary to keep the same benefits
in the package.

The change will, however, result in
an additional deduction of $10
per month from each em-
ployee's paycheck.

If you have any questions,
please contact
me.

Now the sentences become more specific as the paragraph moves along. The reader is not left thinking "Did I miss something?" when the middle of the paragraph becomes overly general. And the unnecessary repetition disappears. In short, the paragraph is better because of its sharper focus.

This same paragraph would work in inductive order, as demonstrated in the following illustration:

In order for
employees at ALFCO
to maintain their current
health benefits, management
has increased the cost of the
benefits package by $10 per month.

The $10 increase will be
added to the current monthly paycheck deduction.

Management has taken this action,
on the advice of the board of directors,
because no other action would allow us to keep
the same level of coverage currently offered by ALFCO.

Management regrets this action but
hopes employees will see it as an expression of
concern and a desire to do all that is possible to
help employees with the ever-increasing health-care costs.

If you have questions, please contact me at your convenience.

Again, the arrangement of the sentences is designed to show the movement of the paragraph from specific to more general statements. The important characteristic of this example paragraph and the example in deductive order is consistency. Sentences follow a logical flow, not a haphazard arrangement.

The following paragraph comes from a letter written to a real-estate agent who handled the sale of a house. The seller discovered after the fact that this sale did not work out as originally intended. Consider the degree to which the illogical order of ideas in the paragraph presents a problem:

101 Pike Road
Montgomery, NC 36064

September 23, 1996

Ms. Jane Spencer
Hallway Realtors, Incorporated
133 Central Avenue
Halisburg, NC 23412

Dear Ms. Spencer:

I am not happy that I am expected to keep a mortgage and insurance in my name on property I no longer own and to which I no longer hold the deed. I need you to restructure the agreement so Mr. Samuels will assume both in fact and name the responsibility for the insurance and the mortgage on that house. The terms of the sale of the property, located at 126 Ivy Avenue, were to be as follows: The final closing date was June 3, 1996. Mr. Samuels was to assume the first mortgage held by Southern Services Financing. He was to take a second mortgage for the balance of the cost of the house with Hallway Realtors, Incorporated. You referred to this as a wrap mortgage. I have learned since then, however, that a wrap mortgage does not include a first-mortgage assumption. Because you misled me during our negotiation, I expect you to correct this situation.

Sincerely,

Jason Seller

Jason Seller

The writer certainly has a point to make in this letter; however, the arrangement of the ideas is somewhat random and, therefore, becomes confusing. Specifically, this random order prevents the reader from clearly identifying the problem the writer wishes addressed. The last sentence does indicate what the writer wants from the reader, but the reader, Ms. Spencer, needs a much more focused presentation of the problem and her contribution to creating it before she can take that request seriously. She needs to feel responsible before she will be motivated to act.

This paragraph's main flaw is that it begins with accusatory language but no context. Ms. Spencer would likely handle many real-estate transactions and must not be expected to remember the details of each. While the name in the return address on the envelope might stir her memory, the writer must not take that possibility for granted. Details about the buyer, location of the house, and closing date do appear, but not until after the writer has expressed dissatisfaction and offered a preliminary request for action. A more effective paragraph would proceed in the following order: Set up the basic context; outline the problem; request corrective action. Such a paragraph would read as follows:

101 Pike Road
Montgomery, NC 36064

September 23, 1996

Ms. Jane Spencer
Hallway Realtors, Incorporated
133 Central Avenue
Halisburg, NC 23412

Dear Ms. Spencer:

On June 3, 1996 you handled the sale of my house at 126 Ivy Avenue to Mr. Samuels. According to the terms of the sale, Mr. Samuels was to assume the first mortgage held by Southern Services Financing and take a second mortgage with Hallway Realtors, Incorporated, for the balance of the cost of the house. You referred to this arrangement as a wrap mortgage. Since then I have learned that with a wrap mortgage, the first mortgage and insurance on the house remain in my name. This arrangement is not what I agreed to, and I am not happy that I am expected to keep in my name the first mortgage and insurance on property I no longer own and to which I hold no deed. Because you misled me during our negotiation, I expect you to correct this situation by restructuring the agreement so Mr. Samuels will assume both in fact and name the responsibility for the insurance and first mortgage on that house.

Sincerely,

Jason Seller

Jason Seller

The ideas in this paragraph now proceed in an effective order that moves from general to specific statements. The opening statements about the date, location, and buyer are in one sense very specific. They present the context-setting facts. In terms of the objective of the letter, however, they are rather general because they discuss neither the nature of the problem nor the desired remedy to that problem. On the other hand, the paragraph ends with the specific request the writer is making of the reader. The final sentence also presents the desired result the middle section outlining the problem predicts by discussing the reasons that action by Ms. Spencer is appropriate. We would not be stretching the point, therefore, in saying that this paragraph has all three of the strengths of organization thus far discussed. It has an effective deductive order, it presents information in the order the reader needs it, and the ideas follow in logical, cause-and-effect sequence. This paragraph has two other important features of tight organization. It uses repetition of key words and transitions to tie related ideas together.

Transition and Repetition

To move logically and coherently, paragraphs often need both effective transition words and repetition of key words. Such words are the road map that assures readers they are following the paragraph, understanding the ideas it is presenting, and seeing the logical relationships among those ideas. The words deserving repetition will be obvious to the writer, for they will be the ones conveying the ideas that require the reader's most serious attention. The appropriate transitions, too, should be rather obvious. They will be those that indicate the logical relationships among consecutive ideas in the paragraph. Following is a list of such logical relationships and a partial list of transitions that build them:

Paragraph Transitions

Cause/Effect: therefore, as a result, so,

Chronology: next, then, after, first, second, finally

Contrast: however, on the other hand, whereas

Similarity: moreover, also, likewise

Illustration: for example, for instance

Definition: in other words, restated, succinctly

Although this list of transitions is by no means complete, it suggests the number of words available to a writer to pull related ideas in a paragraph together, allowing important relationships to become clear to the reader.

Let's look at a paragraph that would be stronger with effective transitions and repetition of key words:

Between 1990 and 1995, the Jonestown branch of Shopway Retail Stores enjoyed an 8 percent average annual increase in gross revenue. Since 1996, the average annual increase has been 2 percent. Management at the store believes that this decline has resulted from increased competition. In 1995, two Store-Mart locations opened in Jonestown and began high-visibility advertising. This caused the Jonestown Thrift City store to increase its advertising. The Shopway branch has lost some of its visibility. Management at the Shopway branch knows that advertising inserts in the Sunday newspaper would increase visibility. The question is whether such inserts would attract enough customers and sufficiently increase sales to be affordable.

The paragraph is not without merit. Its primary strength is that the sentences do present ideas in a logical order, even if that order is not signaled by effective transitions. Transitions are particularly important here, however, because of the variety of logical relationships the paragraph contains: chronology, cause/effect (which dominates), and illustration. The paragraph is also potentially confusing because the writer refers to three different stores without particularly distinctive names. The revised paragraph which follows is stronger because it uses transitional words (indicated by italics) as well as repetition of key terms (indicated by boldface type) to pull the ideas in the paragraph together:

Between 1990 and 1995, the Jonestown branch of Shopway Retail Stores enjoyed an 8 percent average annual **increase** in gross revenue. Since 1996, the average annual **increase** has **declined** to 2 percent. Management at the store believes that this **decline** has resulted from new competition. In 1995, *for example,* two Store-Mart locations opened in Jonestown and began high visibility *advertising.* This *advertising* caused the Jonestown Thrift City store to strengthen its promotional efforts. The Shopway branch has, *as a result,* lost some of its **visibility.** Management at the Shopway store knows that advertising inserts in the Sunday newspaper would **increase visibility.** The question, *therefore,* is whether such advertising can attract enough customers and sufficiently strengthen sales to be affordable.

Note also in this revised paragraph how the repeated words—*increase, decline, advertising,* and *visibility*—present the very ideas that are central to the meaning of the discussion, the decrease in visibility and the need to increase revenue. Two of the three transitions—*as a result* and *therefore*—convey the cause-and-effect logic crucial to the whole advertising concept discussed in the paragraph. The transition *for example* signals an important illustration of the writer's point. In short, the order of the sentences, enhanced by transition and repetition, gives the paragraph a focus, thereby helping the reader see exactly what the writer is saying.

Summary

Writing an effective paragraph requires that the writer use many of the same techniques necessary in writing effective sentences: consider the needs of the reader, the requirements of the purpose, and the order in which ideas need expression. Just as a sentence containing more than one idea needs to have those ideas logically related, so, too, do the ideas in a paragraph require an order and connection. With a logical sequence to its sentences, repetition of key terms, and appropriate transitions, a paragraph can have the same characteristics as a tight, focused sentence.

Exercises

I.   **Paragraph Building:**   The following sentences are arranged in random order. In a logical order, however, they would create a focused paragraph from a sales letter offering air-conditioning duct cleaning. Write a paragraph using these sentences in an effective order. After arranging the sentences, you may also need to add appropriate transitions. Read all the sentences before you begin so you will have an idea about the subject of the paragraph.

1.   Perhaps you suffer from these afflictions and make regular visits to your physician seeking relief.

2.   We will be pleased to conduct a no-cost, no-obligation inspection of your air-conditioning ducts.

3.   So you have nothing to lose; call today at 211-9911.

4.   Fatigue, allergies, sinus infections, and a host of other problems can result when ducts are not clean.

5.   You have perhaps seen recent reports on indoor pollution that have explained the health problems resulting from dirty air-conditioning ducts.

6.   The next time you call your physician, make a second call to ACE Air Conditioning and Service.

7.   We also will provide you with a cleaning estimate and a written copy of our guarantee of satisfaction.

8.   Many people ignore these reports because they do not realize how many simple ailments are caused or aggravated by the molds and accumulated dirt that air-conditioning ducts contain.

9. If your ducts contain a buildup of molds and dirt that could be causing health problems, we will be able to show you this contamination.

II. **Paragraph Coherence:** Make any necessary changes in order, transition, and repetition to make the following paragraph work more effectively.

The most common complaint I hear from our clients is that they simply do not understand the point a given letter is attempting to make. The relationship each of us establishes and maintains with our clients will determine whether Spurling Inc. continues to be a viable accounting firm. More and more, I hear that poorly written letters are creating problems with those relationships. Twice this week, a client has called me about the "arrogance" of a member of Spurling's staff. I then discovered that that "arrogance" surfaced in the tone of a letter. I know full well that no one intended to sound arrogant. Perhaps we would all do well to pay more attention to our writing. Let's all keep in mind that we work for our clients and that they have the right to expect well-written and gracious letters from us.

III. **Inductive and Deductive Order:** Select one of the following writing assignments and prepare a deductive-order paragraph response.

1. Write to a charity that has solicited a contribution and to which you have given in the past, indicating that you will not be able to help because of current financial concerns.

2. Assume that you have been applying for scholarships from organizations in your hometown that sponsor college students. One that you received was from the Chamber of Commerce. Initially, you accepted it but since then have qualified for a larger stipend from your school. To accept this larger award, you cannot be receiving other assistance. Write to your hometown Chamber, declining its offer.

Now select one of the following topics and write an inductive-order paragraph response.

1. Select a charity with which you are familiar and write a mass-mailing letter in which you solicit contributions by stressing the fine work that charity does.

2. You have heard that your hometown Chamber of Commerce offers scholarships to qualified college students. The process begins with your requesting information on the scholarship and introducing yourself to the Chamber's selection committee. Write a letter in which you accomplish both tasks. Be sure that in writing this letter you keep the inductive order by deciding how to fuse both objectives in your first sentences.

CHAPTER VI

Writing Business Letters

Overview

*T*he manner in which we transmit business letters has changed significantly during the past few years. We can now fax letters or send them by a variety of computer on-line services so they arrive promptly, or we can continue to send them through the postal service as in the past. What has not changed, despite the method of transmittal, are the approaches to format and content appropriate to the many types of letters we write to conduct business. In this chapter we will examine the proper ways to set up a business letter and the style, organization, and content of several of the most common letters written to serve a business purpose, both professional and personal. With this chapter we will begin to apply to actual writing situations the vocabulary, sentence structure, adaptation, and organization skills covered in the first five chapters. The exercises at the end of the chapter will give you the opportunity to practice writing the types of business letters examined here.

Formats for Business Letters

All business letters should contain six basic elements: heading, inside address, salutation, body, closing, and signature.

Elements of a Business Letter

1. Heading

2. Inside Address

3. Salutation

4. Body

5. Closing

6. Signature

Some letters place added notations at the end to indicate the typist, if other than the writer; enclosures, if sent with the letter; and other persons to whom a copy of the letter has been sent, if any. The required elements can be arranged in three different formats: full block, modified block, and indented style. Generally, full block or modified block are used in official business correspondence, while persons writing to conduct personal business will use either a modified block or indented format. An example of each format follows.

Most businesses use official letterhead stationery (with the letterhead replacing the heading) and the full-block format illustrated by the following example:

ARDOL Manufacturing
1432 Cameron Street N.W.
Suite 23
Pierce-Burlongs, CA 30435

March 3, 1996

Ms. Janet Galveston
State Health Planning Agency
P. O. Box 3454
Sacramento, CA 32423

Dear Ms. Galveston:

I wish to express my thanks for your sending me a copy of the
State Health Planning Agency's recent report, "Employee Safety
in California." I have examined the recommendations in the
report and concur that businesses in California are responding
well to employee-safety issues. Certainly, we at ARDOL
Manufacturing consider employee safety a top priority and were
pleased to assist with this project.

Again, my thanks for your consideration. Please feel free to
contact me anytime I or my colleagues can help you with future
projects.

Sincerely,

Jarred Phelps
Human Resources Director

JP/rws

This full-block format looks particularly attractive with letterhead
stationery, as each part of the letter aligns with the left margin. However, the modified-block format is also acceptable:

ARDOL Manufacturing
1432 Cameron Street N.W.
Suite 23
Pierce-Burlongs, CA 30435

March 3, 1996

Ms. Janet Galveston
State Health Planning Agency
P. O. Box 3454
Sacramento, CA 32423

Dear Ms. Galveston:

I wish to express my thanks for your sending me a copy of the
State Health Planning Agency's recent report, "Employee Safety
in California." I have examined the recommendations in the
report and concur that businesses in California are responding
well to employee-safety issues. Certainly, we at ARDOL
Manufacturing consider employee safety a top priority and were
pleased to assist with this project.

Again, my thanks for your consideration. Please feel free to
contact me anytime I or my colleagues can help you with future
projects.

Sincerely,

Jarred Phelps
Human Resources Director

JP/rws

The only difference between the full-block and modified-block
formats is that with modified block, the date, closing, and signature
are indented to the right-hand side of the page. Both serve the needs
of professional correspondence.

For personal business correspondence, the modified-block and indented formats are appropriate. For a writer who has a personal letterhead, the modified block would be the appropriate format. One
who does not have personal stationary might choose the indented

format. If our previous example letter had involved a personal thank you, Ms. Galveston would have perhaps received the following letter with an indented format.

---

909 Windsor Avenue
Pierce-Burlongs, CA 30435

March 3, 1996

Ms. Janet Galveston
State Health Planning Agency
P. O. Box 3454
Sacramento, CA 32423

Dear Ms. Galveston:

I wish to express my thanks for your sending me a copy of the State Health Planning Agency's recent report, "Employee Safety in California." I have examined the recommendations in the report and concur that businesses in California are responding well to employee-safety issues. Certainly, I consider safety a top priority for manufacturing firms and, despite my being retired, was pleased to assist with this project.

Again, my thanks for your consideration. Please feel free to contact me anytime I can help you with future projects.

Sincerely,

Jarred Phelps

The indented format, which employs indented paragraphs and is demonstrated here, is probably the least used in business correspondence. The most used is full block; therefore, all examples presented in this chapter follow this preferred format.

Letter of Inquiry

The letter of inquiry is one of the most common letters a person writes, both for professional and personal business. It is an uncomplicated letter; however, we should never assume that it requires any less care than other forms of correspondence. Even the letter of inquiry involves persuading someone to reply. In some cases, readers are anxious to reply because doing so will enable them to conduct business from which they benefit. In other situations, readers will see no tangible benefits to themselves by responding to a query. If the writer is requesting information that is in any way sensitive, a reader might even see some benefit to not responding. Such readers will need particular persuasion.

The easiest way to prompt a reader to respond to a letter of inquiry is to make responding easy. We can make responding easy by writing so what we are seeking is clear. If more persuasion is necessary, we can provide it by establishing why we are making the request generally and why we are making it of our reader specifically. These three elements of a letter of inquiry give us a necessary outline to that letter's contents:

Letter of Inquiry: Contents

1. Provide a cordial opening.

2. Make the specific request or requests.

3. Tell why you are making the request(s).

4. Tell why you are making the request(s) of your reader.

5. Close the letter politely.

To develop these four elements of the letter of inquiry effectively, you can employ the following writing strategy using skills we have practiced in the previous chapters of this book:

Letter of Inquiry: Writing Strategy

1. Keep a cooperative tone so the letter is friendly.

2. Use deductive order by making specific requests early in the letter.

3. Use active voice to keep the **I** and **you** pronouns appropriate to your tone.

4. Employ short sentences that make your requests clear.

Notice how the contents of the letter and the approach to writing it outlined here work together. For example, you want to make your specific requests clear and easy to respond to, so you place them early in the letter (by using deductive order) and present them in short, readable sentences. You create an **I** and **you** communication by stressing the elements of cooperative tone and employing active voice verbs. With all business letters, you will be able to create just such a synthesis between what you need to say and how best to say it. Let's look at an example of a letter of inquiry that combines both elements effectively.

CLARK PUBLISHING, INC.
432 Smithson Street SE
Clifton, NC 23232

July 14, 1996

Mr. Jarvis Bridges, Proprietor
The York Inn
7 High Street
York, England WC1 129

Dear Mr. Bridges:

I shall soon be spending three nights in York conducting business and look forward to visiting a city about which I have heard so many wonderful things. My colleague in York, Mr. Philip Lawson, has recommended The York Inn, and I write requesting information about your policies.

1.   Do you have a single room with facilities available September 24-26, 1994?

2.   What will be the nightly rate for such a room, and do you require an advance deposit?

3.   Do you accept payment by MasterCard?

I need this information in order to process a travel request with my company. I felt, however, that rather than trust a travel guide for this information, I would receive the most prompt and accurate information by writing directly to you. I appreciate your help with this request.

Sincerely,

Janet Blimshey

Janet Blimshey

JB/nms

This letter of inquiry has all the required elements to be effective. The numbered requests for information make responding easy. The polite opening compliments both the hotel and the city in which it is located, while the discussion after the requests makes clear why the writer needs the information in order to stay at the reader's establishment. While hotels respond to such queries as a matter of policy, this one is written to ensure that the response will give the writer precisely what she needs.

Good- and Bad-News Letters

Writing good news might seem a simple process, while writing to give bad news might seem a difficult one. Neither letter presents such a one-dimensional task. Writing good news in a way that enhances the positive is sometimes difficult. Presenting bad news is not as difficult as it might seem if the writer follows a few specific guidelines and uses sound judgment about how to approach the reader. Let's begin with the seemingly more difficult of the two letters.

No one can work in business without at some point having to give bad news, often in writing. However, such situations do not have to end or sour professional relationships or prevent the writer and reader from working effectively together in the future. One of the main characteristics of an effective bad-news letter is that it does not contain a protracted discussion of a straightforward situation. The reader who sees such a letter ramble will actually be more likely to suspect that the writer is *not* saying something. A bad-news letter should, therefore, contain only the following information:

Bad-News Letter: Contents

1. Provide a gentle opening.

2. Explain the situation that led to the bad news.

3. Give the bad news.

4. Offer suggestions that might encourage the reader, if it is possible to do so without sounding condescending.

5. Close the letter politely.

When providing an explanation for the bad news or offering any appropriate suggestions, the writer must be particularly careful not to sound defensive or condescending. Both sections of the letter give the writer a chance to maintain good relations with the reader, but not if the discussion becomes so long that it suggests the writer is avoiding the point. Nor should these sections confuse the reader about the actual message in the letter.

The writing strategy that the writer employs also must be appropriate to the situation. When giving bad news, the writer especially wants to avoid language that can inflame the situation. The following strategy is effective:

Bad-News Letter: Writing Strategy

1. Keep an objective tone.

2. Use inductive-order organization to lead up to the specific message.

3. Use positive passive voice to keep the focus off the writer and on the message.

4. Use third-person pronouns when possible.

5. Use dependent clauses to create cause-and-effect logic that will help the reader understand the reason for the bad news.

The most important part of this strategy is the use of objective tone. The less the writer infuses emotion in a bad-news letter through language, the more likely that letter is to be effective. Let's consider the following example, which follows from the letter of inquiry we saw earlier:

> The York Inn
> 7 High Street
> York, England WC1 129
> Established 1823   J. Bridges, Proprietor
>
> July 20, 1996
>
> Ms. Janet Blimshey
> Clark Publishing, Inc.
> 432 Smithson Street SE
> Clifton, NC 23232
> U.S.A.
>
> Dear Ms. Blimshey:
>
> I write in response to your kind letter of July 14, 1996, requesting information about The York Inn. Sadly, the week of September 24, when you plan to visit, The British Manufacturing Associates Convention is being held in York. As a result, The York Inn has no available rooms. In fact, a waiting list has been established for every night that week in the event of a cancellation. Your name could be added to that list, or you might inquire with the York Visitors' Bureau at 12 River Street.
>
> I hope you will be able to find accommodations in York and that perhaps on some future visit you will remember The York Inn.
>
> Sincerely,
>
> *J. Bridges*
>
> J. Bridges, Proprietor

This letter works for two primary reasons. The tone is cordial and makes clear to Ms. Blimshey that her letter was received with interest. The explanation for the bad news and the effort to offer helpful suggestions both indicate Mr. Bridges' genuine interest in helping her. While his primary purpose was to inform her that he would not have a room available, his secondary purpose of winning a future client is well served. Given this letter, she might well try The York Inn on a future visit.

Writing bad-news letters poses obvious difficulties. Those confronting the writer giving good news are less obvious. First, the writer giving good news may wish to enjoy that news with the reader. In such a situation, however, the writer may detract from the message by becoming too personally involved with presenting it. On the other hand, the writer does not want to become so detached that the impact good news should have is diminished. Clearly, writing good news requires an effective balance between the information being given and the manner of giving it.

First, let's consider what a good-news letter should say:

Good-News Letter: Contents

1. Open with a positive statement.

2. Give the specific good-news message.

3. Provide reasons behind the message.

4. Establish a future relationship between the writer and reader.

5. Close the letter.

If well written, this letter will stress the good-news message and the reasons for it. To spend too much time on other parts of the message, such as the future relationship, would be to diminish the impact of the good news and thus detract from the primary purpose of the letter. The best way for the writer to be involved in such a letter is through an effective writing strategy:

Good-News Letter: Writing Strategy

1. Employ a cooperative tone.

2. Use deductive-order organization to put the specific good-news message early in the letter.

3. Use active voice to stress positive verbs.

4. Use second-person pronouns to keep the focus on the reader.

5. Consider using dependent clauses to keep the cause-and-effect relationship on the reasons behind the good news.

Using this strategy will enable the writer to keep the emphasis on the message while also making the reader feel positive about the person delivering the good news. The result will be an ongoing positive relationship between the two. Consider the following example:

THE JOURNEY'S END MOTEL
182-A Carpenter Street, N.W.
Andersonville, MN 54678

November 14, 1994

Mr. Joseph Delpin
121 Lancer Lane
Milton, MN 56747

Dear Mr. Delpin:

I have reviewed carefully your recent complaint about the Reservations Service of The Journey's End Motel and find that you have identified a serious problem for us. Not only do I plan to change some of our procedures and expand our training of reservations agents, but I ask that you accept the enclosed vouchers to use at any of our motels throughout the U.S. as compensation for your difficulty.

What I specifically found as a result of your contacting me was that our agents were not sufficiently familiar with various special discounts we offer and that we are not sufficiently staffed during peak business hours. Your willingness to contact me about such problems will enable us to provide better service in the future. I certainly hope you will take advantage of our improved efforts.

Again, I appreciate your assistance. If I can ever serve you again, please do not hesitate to contact me.

Sincerely,

Rhenda Jamison

Rhenda Jamison
Operations Director

Enclosure

RJ/nmj

This letter works for two reasons. First, the writer keeps the emphasis on the good news by constantly showing the results of the complaint made by Mr. Delpin. Part of the good news is the motel's effort to compensate him with vouchers. He is probably more concerned with the fact that his complaint received serious attention. This is the best news in the letter; thus it dominates the message. The letter also makes a short, but effective, statement about the future relationship between the writer and the reader. Mr. Delpin is encouraged to continue to patronize the motel. He is also invited to contact Ms. Jamison in the future, if necessary. Such an invitation may be a matter of protocol, but here it is especially effective given the tone and message contained in the letter. Perhaps most important, this letter does not read like a form reply to a complaint but, rather, gives good news in a way as to ensure a strong business relationship in the future.

Complaint Letters

Complaint letters are sometimes necessary when a business situation, whether personal or professional, is not working. They are, therefore, written under difficult circumstances. The purpose of the letter, however, is to help resolve the problem, not to inflame it. Given the conditions under which such letters are written, the writer is particularly challenged to prepare a letter that helps, rather than hurts, a bad situation. Given this fact, the writer must pay particular attention to what such a letter should, and should not, say and to the language used to deliver the message.

Let's consider first what a complaint letter should say. This outline is for a *first* complaint letter (with the hope that a second one will not be necessary):

Complaint Letter: Contents

1. Provide an opening that explains the problem situation.

2. Give the specifics of the problem.

3. Explain why you are dissatisfied.

4. Identify what must be done to resolve the problem.

5. Provide a polite closing.

An effective complaint letter will be particularly attentive to describing the specifics of the problem and what must be done to resolve it. Otherwise, all the reader will see in the letter is an unhappy or dissatisfied person. If the reader is confused about the nature of the problem or what action to take, then the letter will fail and simply contribute to a continued difficult situation.

The writer also will want not to contribute to the problem by employing an ineffective writing strategy. The following strategy can be effective with a complaint letter:

Complaint Letter: Writing Strategy

1. Maintain an objective tone.

2. Use inductive-order organization to lead up to the specific statements about the problem and a suitable remedy.

3. Use active voice to be clear about who should do what to resolve the problem.

4. Rely on dependent clauses to establish cause-and-effect relationships.

The most important part of this strategy is the objective tone. In many complaint letters, the reader is either directly or indirectly responsible for the problem the writer is describing or is the person in the best position to solve that problem. That fact, presented clearly, will get a responsible reader's attention. The writer does not have to use language in a subjective manner to prompt such a reader, certainly not in a first letter presenting a complaint. The following letter provides an example of how to register a complaint and request that action be taken to address a problem.

PARKER MANUFACTURING, INC.
23 Industrial Park Blvd.
P.O. Box 43
Cranston, Alabama 32367

November 14, 1996

Mr. Frederick P. Fowles, Operations Supervisor
Cecil Tool and Dye Company
1895 Waterson Avenue
Cranston, Alabama 34256

Dear Mr. Fowles:

The past two cylinder parts shipments that Parker
Manufacturing has received from Cecil Tool and Dye have
been late. As a result, we have had considerable down time at
some cost to the company. I write to see if we can resolve this
difficulty.

On October 14, 1996, we received a shipment and another on
November 6, 1996. Our contract with Cecil Tool and Dye
specifies, however, that all cylinder parts shipments are to
arrive on the first day of each month. On neither occasion
were we alerted that shipments would be late or given an
explanation why they had not arrived on time.

Because we maintain a limited inventory of parts used in our
manufacturing process, late shipments quickly mean we must
shut down our assembly lines. We are not comfortable
sending employees home on such occasions, and any delays in
our process will lead to delays for our customers.

I am sure this letter will serve as a reminder about the
important relationship between our two companies and the
need that future shipments arrive at the first of the month. I
appreciate your help resolving this matter.

Sincerely,

J. Clifton Ellis

J. Clifton Ellis
Production Supervisor

JCL/nm

The strength of this letter is that it makes clear the serious problem Mr. Ellis' company faces without being threatening. In most cases, this letter would serve its purpose. Consider, however, what would happen should the problem of late shipments continue and a second letter be necessary. In such situations, the letter can make another point by indicating what the writer intends to do if the problem described continues. Then the complaint letter might read as follows:

PARKER MANUFACTURING, INC.
23 Industrial Park Blvd.
P.O. Box 43
Cranston, Alabama 32367

December 11, 1996

Mr. Frederick P. Fowles, Operations Supervisor
Cecil Tool and Dye Company
1895 Waterson Avenue
Cranston, Alabama 34256

Dear Mr. Fowles:

On November 14, I contacted you to report Parker
Manufacturing had received two late cylinder parts shipments
from Cecil Tool and Dye. As I stated then, we had
experienced considerable down time at some cost to the
company. Unfortunately, the most recent shipment, due
December 1, 1996, arrived three days late. Again, we were
not alerted that a shipment would be late or given an
explanation why it had not arrived on time.

I wish to stress that we maintain a limited inventory of parts
used in our manufacturing process and that late shipments
quickly mean we must shut down our assembly lines. We are
now having to delay shipments to our own customers.

At this point, I must remind you of the terms of our contract.
In the event that delays in your shipments create costs for
Parker Manufacturing, the burden for assuming those costs
would rest with your company. My purpose in writing is to
try to resolve this problem. However, if we continue to
receive shipments late, we will be obligated to ask you to
assume responsibility for penalty payments that our customers
expect when we are not able to meet our obligations. We will
also have to look for another supplier for cylinder parts.

I hope that we are able to avoid these time-consuming and
costly problems.

Sincerely,

J. Clifton Ellis

J. Clifton Ellis
Production Supervisor

JCL/nm

This letter still maintains an overall objective tone. And the threat to invoke the terms of the contract between the two companies is clear but not overstated. Therefore, the focus of the letter remains on the writer's desire to resolve the problem. Certainly the first two complaint letters in such a situation should keep this focus. A third letter would tend no longer to be a complaint letter but, rather, a notice of action.

Collection Letters

Collection letters are a routine part of business. Although most loans are paid according to a set schedule so no letter is necessary for individual payments, communication can become necessary when payments do not arrive according to that schedule. The writer must remember, however, that many things can happen to a payment. The most obvious is that it can be lost in the mail. In fact, more often than not late payments result from perfectly understandable situations. Therefore, a collection letter must not become a complaint letter or take an accusatory approach. Sadly, we often see collection letters do just that.

An effective collection letter, or at least a first letter, should simply alert the reader that a payment did not arrive and offer a reminder of the important facts regarding an overdue payment. The following approach to a collection letter will serve this purpose:

Collection Letter: Contents

1. Provide a gentle opening.

2. Set the facts of the debt/payment situation.

3. Identify the fact that a payment is late.

4. Request payment and late fee, if applicable.

5. Close politely.

Most of this information is direct and simple to provide. The one area that might create problems is when the writer reminds the reader of the basic facts of the debt or payment. To dwell on this part of the letter would risk creating a condescending tone in the letter. Careful attention to this part of the letter and the following writing strategy will allow the writer to avoid such a weakness:

Collection Letter: Writing Strategy

1. Establish a cooperative tone.

2. Use deductive-order organization to lead up to the specific request for payment.

3. Use active voice that allows a friendly **I** and **you** pronoun reference.

4. Use short sentences to keep a statement-of-fact style.

Once again, tone is the primary concern in this letter. The writer is much more likely to receive a response to a collection letter, while maintaining cordial business relations with the reader, if the tone of such a letter is not threatening. The following example collection letter maintains a positive tone without compromising the request for the late payment:

CENTRAL SOUTH BANK
Loan Division
1616 Commerce Street N.W.
Canyon City, CO 78912

September 23, 1996

Mr. Andrew S. Claiborn
14 Century Street
Canyon City, CO 78912

Dear Mr. Claiborn:

I write regarding the home-improvement loan that you have with Central South Bank. Your monthly payments on this loan are $125 and are due on the first day of each month. The extended deadline for payment is the 15th of each month. Our records indicate that your September payment has not arrived. We have thoroughly reviewed our records to be sure that we did not make a mistake crediting your account on this loan.

Perhaps this payment has been misplaced or somehow been delayed. However, I ask that you remit this payment and the 2 percent late charge, making the total due $127.50.

I appreciate your attending to this matter. Please let me know if I can be of assistance.

Sincerely,

Craig Dawson
Loan Officer

Even this letter does not totally avoid the possibility of making the reader uncomfortable. However, that discomfort results from the situation in which the collection letter is written, not from the content or tone of the letter itself. Even the most careful writer cannot make such situations completely comfortable. However, this letter is sufficiently fact oriented that the reader would not react negatively to the writer, which is important in such situations.

A follow-up collection letter can be even more difficult to write. That difficulty arises from the fact that a first letter received no response. The writer cannot assume, therefore, that the reader is unaware of the problem because of a lost payment. Rather, the situation would seem to be one in which the reader is, for some reason, having difficulty making a payment. Some companies will at this point use the services of a collection agency. Others will send the follow-up letter, which is a preferred course of action when such a letter can be expected to have results. Again, a nonthreatening tone is important. However, a second letter needs to make a more direct appeal for payment and possibly point out the course of action that will be taken should the second collection letter not produce results:

CENTRAL BANK SOUTH
Loan Division
1616 Commerce Street N.W.
Canyon City, CO 78912

October 1, 1996

Mr. Andrew S. Claiborn
14 Century Street
Canyon City, CO 78912

Dear Mr. Claiborn:

On September 23, 1996, I contacted you to report that the September payment on your home-improvement loan with Central Bank South was late. I have not received a response, nor has the bank received that payment of $127.50. Your October payment is now due.

The terms of your loan with Central Bank South stipulate that should you miss two consecutive payments, your loan will be considered in default. At that time, I will be forced to cash the bonds you deposited as collateral on this loan. Your October payment will not be considered late until October 15, 1996. I ask that you make both your September and October payments by that date.

I hope that we can avoid declaring your loan in default by your prompt response to this notice.

Sincerely,

Craig Dawson
Loan Officer

This is an appropriate follow-up collection letter. It reminds the reader of the terms of his contract and specifies what action the bank can and will take in accord with those terms. The tone remains nonthreatening. The threat of action is described within the context of the contractual responsibility Mr. Claiborn assumed when he took the loan. This direct, objective approach, even in a second letter, is appropriate.

Claims Letters

All businesses expect to deal with claims made against their defective products and unsatisfactory services. The more effective the letter, however, the more likely a writer is to see a claim acted on properly and in timely fashion. A business is much more likely to respond to a claim based on fact rather than on emotion. Therefore, a valid claim, one that has the facts behind it, should avoid emotion that might obscure those facts. A claims letter also should be organized so those facts have impact. An effective organization for stressing the facts would be as follows:

Claims Letter: Contents

1. Provide a polite opening that sets the context for the claim.

2. Make a specific request or claim.

3. Give the background information about why you are making the request. Be sure to identify the problem leading to the claim.

4. Offer a goodwill closing.

Clearly the crucial part of this letter is using facts in the section that describes the background situation. Facts should refer to a company's policies, its guarantee on a product, or normal expectations of satisfaction with a product or service. A claim based simply on the writer's deciding against a purchase or deciding not to conduct business would be weak, although some money-back guarantees might allow this option as well.

A claims letter will also benefit from a strong writing strategy. An appropriate strategy would be one in which language does not call attention to itself but, rather, accents the factual statements made by the writer. Toward that end, a writer should employ the following guidelines:

Claims Letter: Writing Strategy

1. Maintain an objective tone.

2. Organize material in a deductive order that makes a specific request early in the letter.

3. Use active voice to accent verbs since you are seeking action.

4. Employ second-person pronouns to stress that you expect the reader to act.

5. Consider effective dependent clauses to highlight cause-and-effect relationships.

Two parts of this writing strategy are particularly important. The objective tone will help keep attention on the facts in the claim. The use of second-person pronouns will alert the reader, the *you* in the letter, that you, the writer, expect a response to your claim.

A first claims letter does not always produce the intended results, and a second letter may become necessary. However, one written in the manner of the following example may help avoid that difficulty:

                              Janet H. Hodges
                       12-A Apartment Building C
                            Ridgeview Heights
                            3234 Highline Drive
                            Shipton, NY 34876

March 4, 1996

Mr. Peter Sardeven
Claims Department
Computers By Mail, Inc.
P. O. Box 34567
Albertson, WI 65712

Dear Mr. Sardeven:

I have been purchasing computer equipment from your
firm for several years and now must, unfortunately,
ask for your assistance with the IQC 486, which
arrived today.

Specifically, I refer to your guarantee of an on-
site visit to repair any equipment that does not
arrive in proper working order. Please contact your
service contractor in the Shipton, New York, area,
and have that contractor call me as soon as possible
to schedule a repair visit.

On February 16, 1996, I used the Computers By Mail
800 number to order the IQC 486. I arranged payment
on my MasterCard. I have already been billed for and
paid that charge. The IQC 486 arrived today;
however, the hard drive appears not to work properly.
I have been unable to load any of my software. I have
considerable computer experience but have found no
way to solve the problem; therefore, I assume that
the difficulty is mechanical.

I have always thought your guarantee was a major
attraction to conducting business with Computers By
Mail and certainly plan to continue to do so. However,
I need this unit operating as soon as possible and am
sending this letter overnight delivery for that reason.
I shall look forward to hearing from you or your
service contractor as soon as possible.

Sincerely,

Janet Hodges

Janet H. Hodges

The claim made in this letter might be one effectively handled by telephone. However, if Ms. Hodges wants a record of her efforts to resolve her claim, a letter serves that purpose. Such records are important when companies do not act on claims in an appropriate fashion. Then the person making the claim may need to look into legal action requiring a record of efforts made to resolve a claim without such action. However, a well-written claims letter can often resolve these types of problems without the time and expense of legal action becoming necessary.

Summary

The letters discussed in this chapter constitute much of the correspondence needed to conduct business, both professional and personal. With each, we have looked not only at the content and organization they require but at an appropriate writing strategy as well. Writers should always remember that they must pay as much attention to how they present a message as they do to what that message contains. This ability to apply basic principles of style and organization is a primary characteristic of a strong writer and is one of the most sought-after skills in the business world today. Often, a potential employer first detects this ability in the application letter and resume a potential employee submits. Because these two documents are so important, they receive detailed discussion in the next chapter.

Exercises

Whenever necessary to use proper business-letter form with the following exercises, create addresses, dates, titles, etc.

I. **Letter of Inquiry:** You are the Local Arrangements Coordinator for the upcoming convention of the Southeastern Accountants Association, which plans to meet in Atlanta, Georgia. The association has 2,546 members, and past events have attracted on average 75 percent of the membership, with 50 percent of these bringing a spouse or guest. The convention will last four days and conduct 26 sessions each day. Consider what types of facilities the organization will need, and query the Convention Bureau in Atlanta about hotels that could host this activity.

II.   Good- and Bad-News Letter: Write the appropriate letter for each of the following scenarios:

1.   You are a loan officer for Amherst Savings, Inc., and have completed processing a loan application from Mr. Lonnie Jacobs. Mr. Jacobs sought a loan of $25,000. He offered to secure the loan using his house as collateral. Your investigation showed that Mr. Jacobs owes $56,000 on his house, valued at $65,000. You also found his credit report listed him to owe $4,000 on his MasterCard, which allows a credit line of only $3,000. Write Mr. Jacobs a letter denying his credit application.

2.   You are the Human Resources Director for Sterling Associates, a financial services firm in your area. Sterling Associates has a program that allows members of the staff to apply for tuition assistance in the event that they want to return to school. Mr. Harris Dawson, who has an associates degree and works in computer programming for the company, has applied for this award and proposed returning to school to complete a four-year degree in information systems. The review of his application found that he is highly recommended by fellow employees, conscientious about his work, and extremely capable as a programmer. The award will pay for all fees and books, as well as 100 percent tuition for courses in which he earns an *A*, 80 percent for a *B*, and 60 percent for a *C*. The one condition is that Mr. Dawson remain with the company at least two years after completing his degree. Write the letter giving Mr. Dawson the good news.

III.   Complaint Letter: You are a senior at your institution attempting to graduate at the end of the next quarter or semester. Your major (use your own) has several required courses. During this quarter, you attempted to register for the last two of these, neither of which will be offered again before your desired graduation date. By the time you were cleared for registration, both classes were closed. You saw the instructors for these courses and the department head, but no one would agree to boost the courses' capacity to let you in. You now face a delayed graduation. Write a complaint letter to the appropriate dean at your school to complain. You may want to review information in your school's catalog about commitment to the student, and so on, to use in this letter. And you have several approaches that would be appropriate (that the classes are seldom offered, that they are required for graduation, and so forth). This letter can work, despite the fact your efforts have been frustrated so far, so use your best judgment when planning and writing.

IV. **Collection Letter:** Assume for this exercise that your school has a tuition payment plan that allows students to pay half their tuition the day they register and the other half on or before mid-term. The school policy is that a student who fails to make the second payment will be dropped from the class roll(s) for all classes. You are the Assistant Bursar at your school and are writing to all students who have failed to make the second payment. Mr. Harold Davis owes $435 and is now one week in default. If he makes that payment within two weeks, his name will be added to the final-grade sheet sent to the instructor. If not, he will not receive credit for the course. Write this collection letter.

V. **Claims Letter:** Three weekends ago, you were in New Orleans. While there, you purchased an Indian bedspread in an expensive but poorly lit shop, Imports Unlimited, on Jackson Square. Later, you washed it according to the instructions on the attached tab, but when you put the spread back on your bed, you noticed that the dye had run, making the pattern uneven. You remember that the shop had a sign posted stating that merchandise could not be refunded but assumed that this policy did not apply to defective merchandise. A return to New Orleans to replace the spread is not practical, but you are willing to return it by mail if you receive a refund. The spread cost $200. Write a letter requesting a refund and promising to return the spread after receiving notice that your claim will be honored.

VI.   Use Your Judgment: In this letter, you should use your own judgment about how to proceed. You are the owner of Imports Unlimited and have received the complaint letter described in the prior exercise. You note the description of the defective bedspread, but you also know that handmade Indian fabrics are often irregular. You also know you have a sign posted that says you do not give refunds on purchases. You are willing to exchange merchandise for cause when that merchandise is returned. Remembering that your business is driven by goodwill with tourists, write back and indicate that you cannot refund the purchase price but will consider an exchange if the customer can return with the defective spread and select a new one.

CHAPTER
VII

Writing for Employment

Overview

*T*he professional documents we write when seeking employment are among the most important we will prepare in our careers. Unfortunately, far too many job-seekers produce letters and resumes that do not reflect their ability and experience. Such applicants are often well prepared to handle the responsibilities of the positions for which they apply but simply fail to demonstrate that fact when they write a job-application letter or set up a resume.

We must begin by understanding the process of getting a job and how our communication efforts fit into that process. First, we have to capture our potential employers' interest and convince them they are not wasting time by considering us for a position. Second, we have to provide details about our abilities in a form that makes them want to meet us in a personal interview. Once we get the interview, then we are in a position to secure the job.

The job-application letter is successful if it gets an employer to read our resumes. Resumes are successful if they generate enough interest that employers want to meet us. The interview allows us to demonstrate that claims made in our letters and resumes are valid. Unfortunately, too many people try to go straight from letter to job offer. They try, in other words, to make the letter and resume do more than is possible and, as a result, both fail.

Application Letters

What does one say in a job-application letter? This question causes many applicants to pause, but it should not. Potential employers tell applicants what to say; they make clear what they want in an application

123

letter when writing the job description for the position announcement. If the announcement does not contain a description, a quick call to a personnel office will often provide one. The bottom line is that a potential employer wants the application letter to repeat what the job description has said, fleshed out with details related to the individual applicant. Let's look at an advertisement for a job that requires certain abilities, none of which are overly specialized:

Help Wanted

DISTRICT MANAGER: Full Time. *The Jonesboro Daily News* has an opening for a District Manager in the Jonesboro area. This position is responsible for the supervision of an all-adult carrier force. Applicants should have some college experience and bookkeeping skills, be neat and dependable, have a good driving record, and be able to work morning hours. Competitive salary, company car, and full benefits. Send application and references to Harold Harris, Human Resources Director, P.O. Box 34, Jonesboro, Alabama 33454.

This job description provides excellent detail for the writer of an application letter to know what to say. The employer will respond positively to the letter if it deals with the following matters:

The applicant is available **full time.**

The applicant is able to **supervise** adults.

The applicant has some **college experience.**

The applicant has **bookkeeping skills.**

The applicant has a **good driving record.**

The applicant is available **morning hours.**

The applicant is **having references sent.**

The employer mentioned these qualifications hoping applicants will have them and mention them in an application letter. Therefore, any letter applying for the job should mention as many of them as possible. The letter need not discuss all these qualifications at length, but, certainly, it should deal with them in enough detail—either directly or indirectly—to make the employer want to read a resume.

Now let's look at a letter that does not take advantage of the job description provided by the employer:

Mr. Harold Harris
P.O. Box 34
Jonesboro, Alabama

Dear Mr. Harris,

I am interested in the position of District Manager for *The Jonesboro Daily News*. In fact, I was a paperboy for the paper for seven years and learned much about the distribution of papers at that time.

I am currently commuting to Wilson, Alabama, to attend State University where I am working on my degree in human resource management. However, the cost of my education is increasing and making it necessary for me to find a full-time job. Because I have lived in the Jonesboro area all my life and worked for the newspaper in the past, I know the routes and the types of problems that arise with unsatisfied customers. By hiring me, you will get someone who can help resolve those problems and be sure that the paper's customers are pleased with the service they receive. I have also taken several accounting courses at State University, as well as courses in my major.

I will be available to go to work immediately and look forward to hearing from you.

Sincerely,

Peter Patterson

Peter Patterson

In this letter, the applicant has not given the employer what he wanted. Consider how many of the items listed in the ad Mr. Patterson did not mention or mentioned too indirectly and too briefly. His opening paragraph suggests that his primary qualification is his having worked as a paperboy for the paper in the past. It does not deal with his ability to supervise, and, by mentioning his college studies, he raises the question of his availability for work. A college student might attend night classes and work during the day, but Mr. Patterson has not said that he is on such a schedule. He does make clear that he has college experience but indicates bookkeeping skills only by an indirect reference to accounting courses.

The letter also makes basic mistakes in format and protocol. It is undated and offers no heading address. The salutation is followed by a comma, not a colon. In short, Mr. Harris will probably not want to interview this applicant for reasons that Mr. Patterson could have controlled. A better response to this ad might read as follows:

Route 1, Box 45
Jonesboro, Alabama 34567

July 30, 1996

Mr. Harold Harris, Human Resources Director
The Jonesboro Daily News
P. O. Box 34
Jonesboro, Alabama 33454

Dear Mr. Harris:

I write to apply for your position of District Manager for *The Jonesboro Daily News*, which I saw advertised in the Sunday, July 27, 1996, edition of the paper. Not only do I have the college experience and bookkeeping skills required for the job, but I previously worked for the paper and understand the task of those carriers I would be supervising.

I am currently commuting to Wilson, Alabama, to attend State University where I am working on my degree in human resource management. Because I take only night classes, my schedule would not interfere with my job as District Manager. In fact, my work at State University has led me to take courses in both management and accounting that would help me with the job. The accounting courses have helped me polish my bookkeeping skills, and, as my resume indicates, I have almost completed my management courses. These courses, combined with my current position as third-shift manager of the Sunshine Inn, give me both the theory and practical experience to work well with adult carriers.

I have lived in Jonesboro all my life. I know the people, the paper's routes, and the types of problems that carriers face. By hiring me, you will get someone who can make sure that customers are satisfied with the service they receive.

I am available to go to work immediately and would appreciate a chance to meet with you at your convenience to discuss my qualifications. I can be reached at (205) 244-3412 and have arranged, in addition to the enclosed resume, to have a copy of my placement file sent to you.

Sincerely,

Peter Patterson

Peter Patterson

Enclosure

As you review this letter, consider the ways it improves on the first effort. It is dated and has an appropriate format. It makes clear that the letter is an application, not merely an expression of interest. It indicates how the applicant learned of the job. The opening paragraph sums up the applicant's *best* qualifications by addressing the issues of supervision and management, as well as bookkeeping. It also deals with the *humanizing* element of his previous employment with the paper, but only after addressing the central issues. It points to the resume, always an essential strategy, and states that the requested placement file is on the way. In short, this letter takes full advantage of the information provided in the job description. After reading this letter, Mr. Harris will probably read Mr. Patterson's resume. If the resume works, an interview could be forthcoming.

Resumes

Let's assume that Mr. Patterson interested the employer enough to get him to read his resume. But an applicant still needs to secure an interview. Therefore, Mr. Patterson's resume must build on the positive first impression created by his letter. To do so, the resume must not only provide the correct information, but it must provide that information in an effective manner.

First, what is a resume, and what can it do for an applicant? It is an item-by-item list of an applicant's qualifications for employment. Generally, these qualifications consist of academic or professional experience but also may include career objectives, research abilities, school and community activities, honors and awards, certifications, and so on. On the resume, an applicant can provide details about qualifications briefly presented in a cover letter that, for the sake of brevity, were not fleshed out. What a resume cannot do, what it should not try to do, is prove that an applicant is a *nice* person. The employer will decide that sort of thing in an interview anyway, not while reading a letter or resume. Thus, a resume should be direct, professional, and focused, focused on qualifications. Several resume formats exist and offer applicants such as Mr. Patterson options for making themselves attractive to a potential employer.

Chronological Format

Although in reverse chronological order, the chronological-format resume is a straightforward presentation of an applicant's work history, education, and personal background. This resume format is traditional and is particularly effective for demonstrating an applicant's growth and development through a series of educational experiences and jobs. The chronological approach also stresses previous employers and job titles, as well as work experience, if providing this information will enhance an applicant's chances of getting a job. Such a format is not effective when the applicant has a spotty work history, with periods of unemployment or frequent changes in employment, or has changed career goals. Used in these situations, the chronological format suggests instability.

The applicant whose qualifications balance education and work experience is a likely candidate for a chronological-format resume, especially in the modified form that follows and that graduating college students might employ:

PETER PATTERSON
Route 1, Box 45
Jonesboro, Alabama 33454
(205) 244-4444

OBJECTIVE
Human Resource Management Position

QUALIFICATIONS
While working as night manager of the Sunshine Inn, I have gained experience supervising a staff, handling inventory, bookkeeping, and developing other management skills. My education has added to these skills through courses in human resource management and accounting.

EDUCATION
B.S. (candidate) Human Resource Management, State University, 3.34 GPA. Degree anticipated June 1996.

WORK EXPERIENCE
Sunshine Inn.   8/91 to Present
NIGHT MANAGER—Responsible for third-shift activities, including registering guests, room maintenance, security, closing the day's accounts, and preparing bank deposits for morning delivery. The Inn has 150 units and daily income of approximately $5,000.

The Jonesboro Daily News.   7/85 to 6/90
ROUTE CARRIER—Responsible for two rural routes, including delivery collections for more than 200 customers. Twice named Carrier of the Month.

ACTIVITIES
Member, Jonesboro United Methodist Church

Active in hunting, fishing, and camping

This resume has a chance of getting Mr. Patterson an interview. The focus is on education generally and experience specifically. Both indicate his management and accounting (bookkeeping) background. The detail on his work as night manager suggests his ability to supervise others, an important concern in the job description to which he is responding. The other details on education, activities, and honors make him appear to be a well-rounded applicant. Because the job description did stress work skills and not education, however, he might have adapted this resume format to more directly stress his experience.

Functional Format

The functional-format resume helps an applicant stress specific skills. Such an approach to a resume is particularly helpful when the applicant is seeking a new type of position where skills, rather than work experience, are the primary qualification. Unlike the chronological format, it does not focus on job titles or previous employers. Rather, it allows the applicant to list in detail those tasks he or she has experience with and is, therefore, qualified to perform for the potential employer. Such a format might not serve Mr. Patterson as well as the chronological format, given the limited experience that appears in the previous example. If, however, he had completed his degree and his experience included more than his night manager position, his functional resume might look like the one that follows:

PETER PATTERSON
Route 1, Box 45
Jonesboro, Alabama 33454
(205) 244-4444

OBJECTIVE
Human Resource Management Position

QUALIFICATIONS
Supervision and Management

Maintained inventory and supplies orders for 150-room motel.

Scheduled a staff of 14 employees and conducted regular performance evaluations.

Prepared an employee performance-evaluation plan adopted by corporate offices of Sunshine Inn for use by all local managers.

Planned several convention and banquet activities for various professional meetings.

Resolved customer complaints and worked with attorneys to resolve liability claims.

Accounting and Finance

Managed annual payroll of approximately $500,000.

Handled annual income records totaling more than $12 million.

Worked with corporate tax accountants on filing all state and federal returns.

EMPLOYMENT
Manager, Sunshine Inn, Jonesboro, Alabama   2/93 to Present

Night Manager, Sunshine Inn, Jonesboro, Alabama   4/91 to 2/93

EDUCATION
M.B.A. State University (1994)

B.S. Human Resource Management, State University (1992)

Actually, with the qualifications in this resume, Mr. Patterson would be overly qualified for the supervisory position described earlier in this discussion of letters and resumes. What we can see clearly here, however, is how the functional format calls attention to the managerial/supervisory and bookkeeping skills that the original job description called for. To draw specific attention to qualifying skills and experience is the reason for shifting from the chronological format to the functional. An extension of this shift is the targeted-format resume.

Targeted Format

The targeted-format resume is much like the functional format and stresses particular qualifications but does so for an applicant who is selective about positions to apply for. The targeted-format resume is appropriate for an applicant seeking a specific type of position and trying to point out how precisely his or her experiences match the requirements for such employment. Often, a well-qualified applicant who wants a similar position with a new or better company will use this style resume. Again, let's add to Mr. Patterson's experience and skills to create an example targeted-format resume:

PETER PATTERSON
Route 1, Box 45
Jonesboro, Alabama 33454
(205) 244-4444

OBJECTIVE
Human Resource Management Position

CAPABILITIES
- Maintain a standard motel staff payroll

- Coordinate convention and tourist activities

- Work with significant income and tax records

- Organize inventory records and supplies orders

- Conduct employee performance evaluations

- Schedule and supervise facility repair and improvement

ACHIEVEMENTS
- Named Outstanding Local Manager for a major motel chain

- Prepared an employee performance-evaluation plan adopted by the corporate offices and used throughout the United States by a major motel chain

- Operated a profitable local unit for a major motel chain for the three years I served as manager

- Supervised a staff of 14 motel workers

- Coordinated with other local motels the American Association of Accountants 1993 convention and banquet that had approximately 1,600 participants

EMPLOYMENT
Manager, Sunshine Inn, Jonesboro, Alabama   2/93 to Present

Night Manager, Sunshine Inn, Jonesboro, Alabama   4/91 to 2/93

EDUCATION
M.B.A. State University (1994)

B.S. Human Resource Management, State University (1992)

Summary

Seeking a job requires many skills, not the least of these being communication skills. First, an applicant must be able to read a job description effectively and use it wisely. The communication skill here is that of a perceptive audience. Then, the applicant must be able to prepare a letter that interests an employer enough to read the applicant's resume. The resume must be structured in the format that best presents the applicant's qualifications. The applicant has several options. The chronological-format resume suits the applicant with limited work experience and educational qualifications. The functional-format resume is more appropriate for the applicant with experience but who is still looking at a variety of positions. The targeted-format resume helps the experienced applicant seeking a specific type of position. With these options available, the most successful applicant is generally the one who has made clear decisions about what he or she wants out of the job search and can structure that search accordingly.

Exercises

I.   **Analyzing a Job Description:**   Study the following job descriptions, and list for each the important statements or qualifications you would want to be sure to take into account in an application letter seeking the positions.

Office Manager: Dawson Temporaries seeks an Office Manager for its Clayton, New York location. Duties include working with local businesses needing temporary help, maintaining accounts, coordinating schedules and assignments for temporaries, and recruiting quality employees. The successful applicant should have some college experience in business-related field and/or experience supervising others. A strong command of accounting/bookkeeping skills necessary. Send letter and resume to Harold Dawson, President, Dawson Temporaries, Inc., P. O. Box 38, Buffalo, NY 34789.

Financial Planner: Williams, Inc., a major investment firm, seeks college graduates to work as financial planners. Any major is acceptable, but some business courses will be an asset. Financial planners work with clients to develop investment strategies and present options deemed by the company's researchers to be secure and potentially profitable. The successful candidate will have computer and communication skills and be able to work well with people. Relocation a strong possibility. Send letter and resume to Edwin Williams, Director of Human Resources, Williams, Inc., P. O. Box 467, Wilson, Delaware 78910.

II. **Preparing a Resume:** Using the example resumes in this chapter, select the type that suits your background and interests, and prepare your own resume. Make sure you provide the needed detail to interest a potential employer in interviewing you. Perhaps you will want to prepare more than one resume before deciding which best reflects your qualifications. Sometimes preparing a resume is simpler when we are responding to a specific job application. Perhaps you will want to use those in the first exercise or to find one from another source to guide you as you prepare your resume. Also take care to follow the examples in resume design so yours is neat and attractive.

III. **Application Letters:** Now use the resume you prepared in the prior exercise and write an application cover letter applying for one of the positions in the first exercise or for the position in the alternative announcement you selected.

CHAPTER VIII

Research and Documentation

Overview

*T*he ability to conduct research and to cite that research when using it in a report is one of the marks of an educated person. During the past few years, however, the process of conducting research has become much more involved than it was in the past because of the development of computer research technology. While this technology has made conducting research more involved, it has made it easier as well. And nothing has changed about how we document research when using it in our reports. Surprisingly, however, we hear more and more about political figures and others who have used in their speeches material taken elsewhere and failed to acknowledge the source. This failure constitutes nothing less than intellectual theft or plagiarism. A professional has no business engaging in such practices, and the ability to avoid such mistakes goes back to documenting a paper submitted as a class assignment. The use and documentation of material in a business report does more than acknowledge sources, however. It lends credibility to the arguments the writer is making, and it gives readers the information they need if they wish to check a writer's source or to read more about the topic of the report. This chapter outlines the basic research procedures and philosophy of documentation and examines the techniques of documentation according to the *MLA Handbook for Writers of Research Papers* (1995), the *Chicago Manual of Style* (1993), and the *Publication Manual of the American Psychological Association* (1994).

Narrowing a Topic

In many classes, students find that they must take a general subject for their writing and narrow that subject to a specific topic. In

137

business writing, the process of narrowing a writing task is somewhat different. A business report is generally a response to a precisely defined problem or need. When this is the case, the topic of the report is already sufficiently narrow when the writer begins to conduct research. In order to establish focus for the research and writing, the writer must consider the different components of the problem, the possible responses to that problem, and the criteria by which the responses can be evaluated. Consider, for example, how a writer might respond to a company's problem with *high absenteeism*. The basic topic already has focus because the writer is limited to researching and discussing the specific problem. The researcher has not begun work narrowing a large subject, such as problems confronting the company, to the specific topic of absenteeism. Rather, the research will break the absenteeism topic down into its components. Here, the best approach would be to narrow the focus by listing the possible causes: illness, child-care problems, elder-care difficulties, poor morale, and so on. With such a list, the writer can begin targeted, thus efficient, research.

Had the specific problem been to determine whether a company should buy or lease automobiles for its company cars, the researcher should use a different approach to narrowing the task. With such a topic, the researcher can create focus by selecting the criteria by which the two options can be compared. Generally speaking, these criteria would be related to the cost of maintaining a company motor pool: initial cost, insurance costs, servicing costs, and so forth. Again, however, the process of narrowing a topic, or giving focus to a task, will leave the research with specific and clearly defined information needs. The next chapter, on business reports, will also show how such decisions about focus are related not just to the manner in which we research reports but to the way we organize them as well.

Researching a Topic

Many businesses today invest considerable capital to build on-site research facilities. Such facilities allow them access to the most up-to-date information available on a variety of topics that can affect the way they conduct business. With such a facility, for example, a construction company bidding on a project in China can quickly access the information necessary to prepare a competitive proposal. With computer link-ups, on-site negotiators can modify bids at a moment's notice. This capacity can make the difference between securing a project worth millions of dollars and losing out on such profitable business. What goes into such a research process, however, is no different than what a student does when conducting library research for a class assignment.

A student conducting research on a business topic—let's use corporate-sponsored day care as an example—has a variety of resources available in any library. From the *reference collection*, the student might find material on state requirements for day-care facilities. The *general collection* would have a variety of books on how to set up a successful program for early childhood care. By using the *periodical collection*, the student could look at articles on successful programs already in place and the costs/savings information resulting from corporate-sponsored day care. Even *government documents* would add information to such a research project. The following lists indicate major titles for business research we can find in these parts of a library collection:

General Business Information: *Encyclopedia of Associations, Industry Norms and Key Business Ratios, MediaMark Research Reports, Standard and Poor's Industry Survey.*

Company Information: *Corporate Directory, Directory of Corporate Affiliations, Million Dollar Directory, Moody's Manual: Bank and Finance, Moody's Manual: Industrial, Moody's Manual: International, Moody's Manual: Municipal and Government, Moody's Manual: Public Utility, Moody's Manual: Transportation, Ward's Business Directory.*

Investments: *Business & Investment Almanac, Moody's Bond Record, Moody's Bond Survey, Moody's Handbook of Common Stocks, Value Line Investment Survey.*

Government Publications: *Economic Censuses, Economic Indicators, Occupational Outlook Handbook, Statistical Abstract of the United States, Survey of Current Business, U.S. Industrial Outlook.*

These titles by no means exhaust the possibilities and do not include the hundreds of periodicals we have access to when researching a business topic. In fact, many business topics deal with issues changing so rapidly that the only way to have up-to-date information is to do a complete search for information in periodicals.

Using Indexes

Most students have used periodical indexes to add sources to a research bibliography, and using those that list business articles is no different from using an index such as *The Reader's Guide*. Some of the most common indexes used in business research include *Accounting & Tax Index*, *Business Periodicals Index*, *Public Affairs Information Service Bulletin*, and *Wall Street Journal and Barron's Index*. To use all of these indexes, we look up our subject—corporate-sponsored day care—in the volumes for the various years. Identifying the proper subject heading is the key to using an index effectively. Topics, however, do not always provide effective subject headings. Probably, we would not find "corporate-sponsored day care" as a subject heading in any index and would have to try "day care" instead. We would also want to check other related headings, such as "child care." The best source of possible subject headings for any topic is *The Library of Congress Subjects Headings List*, which all libraries have and which they use when listing books in their card catalogs.

Finding the correct subject heading can be particularly important when using a computer database such as ABI/Inform or ProQuest to develop a bibliography of periodical articles. Because such searches are taking the place of a review of printed abstracts, we would do well to examine the procedure of searching for sources in such a database. For this example, we will use the procedure for using ABI/Inform, one of the most common databases available and one that lists articles from most of the major periodicals that discuss business topics, including the *Wall Street Journal*.

In most libraries, a computer station will be devoted to ABI/Inform, so loading a disc will not be necessary. Rather, the researcher would begin by using the arrow keys on the keyboard to highlight **ABI/Inform** on the screen, then pressing **Enter.** The screen will then display the prompt **Search Terms:** and a flashing cursor. Next, the researcher enters the proper subject heading—**day care**—and presses **Enter.** The system searches for any articles in the database that use the term **day care** as a descriptor. Once the search is complete, the screen will indicate the number of sources found. To see a list of the titles of these articles, the researcher would press **Enter.** Using the highlight bar, the researcher can move along this list of titles until finding one that looks promising. When the highlight bar is on the promising title, the researcher can press **Enter** to view complete publication information and an abstract. At this point, the researcher can move back to the title list by pressing the **Escape** key, move to the abstract of the next article by pressing **+**, or move to the previous article by pressing **-**. Along the way, abstracts and publication information can be marked for printing or downloading by pressing **F9.**

One problem would have occurred had the researcher begun with the subject **day care.** The number of articles found would be so large, and would include so many articles not really related to the topic of **corporate-sponsored day care,** that reviewing them all would have wasted considerable time. In such situations, the researcher can begin a new search by pressing **F3** and using two terms to narrow the field: **day care** and **corporate.** With this search, only articles that use both terms as descriptors will appear in the final list. Sometimes taking a few minutes to narrow a search can be well worthwhile, for then the final list of periodical articles will be just what the researcher needs.

Organizing Researched Information

Different researchers have different ways to take and organize their notes. What is important is that those notes be organized and that they clearly indicate when a source is being paraphrased and when it is being directly quoted. Because a business report has such a precise pattern of organization, however, organizing notes within that pattern can save time once the actual drafting of the report begins. For example, a business report will begin by defining the *problem* the researcher is attempting to solve. It will discuss *possible actions* that a company can take to solve the problem. The report will use *criteria* to evaluate the appropriateness of those actions. The best way to take and organize notes when conducting research is to use these basic divisions of the report. Earlier in this chapter, we focused on the topic of absenteeism by listing its possible causes: illness, child care, elder care, poor morale. These subdivisions of the problem, or topic, provide a mechanism for organizing information provided by research. The simplest way to use these subtopics to organize notes is to create electronic files on disc. If, for example, the researcher creates a file for each subtopic related to the problem, then any information related to that subtopic can be kept in that file. When the research is completed, these files will already have the information organized to correlate with the organization of the report.

When entering information into electronic files, the researcher must be sure to be accurate about three things. First, quoted material must be so identified and properly distinguished from paraphrased notes. Second, quoted material must be accurate. No researcher should change the wording of material that will later be presented as a direct quotation. Third, all notes, whether quoted or paraphrased, must be kept so their source and the page number in that source are properly identified. Perhaps the best way to keep this connection between note and source is to also keep an electronic file listing in proper bibliographic form and numbering all sources the researcher consults. Then, a simple notation following each note from a sub-topic file will tie that note to a specific source and a page number in that source. Consider the following example:

Notes on Absenteeism and Child Care

"Albertson Industries found that after establishing an on-site day-care program, absenteeism dropped from an average of 8.4 days per employee each year to 4.6 days. This drop led to a savings of more than $450,000 in 1995 as the company used fewer temporary workers and paid less overtime to maintain productivity." (3, p 56)

The quotation marks tell the researcher that the information is quoted directly from the source, something that he or she might not remember later when using the note. The information in parentheses, **(3, p. 56),** indicates that that quotation comes from page 56 in source number 3 in the electronic file listing sources. In short, by using electronic files to take notes, the researcher later finds that information about the subtopics in the report is all kept together and that that information is clearly identified as quoted or paraphrased and as coming from a specific page number in an identified source.

Basic Theory of Documentation

All of the style manuals discussed in this chapter are valid for both academic and professional papers. Each provides the researcher with the means necessary to indicate the source of borrowed material. Generally, this means including with the paper or report either a Works Cited or References page and correlating in-text notes in parentheses with the entries in the Works Cited or References to indicate the source of borrowed material. It can also mean providing numbered endnotes to give the reader that information. In both cases, the mechanics of documentation is not difficult. Sometimes knowing *what* to document is more challenging.

Let's begin by reviewing what *not* to do. Writers should not cite material simply because they learned it for the first time through their research. What needs to be cited is never determined by the knowledge of the researcher before beginning a research project. Writers should not cite material simply to "play it safe" and avoid *plagiarism*. Clearly, we want to avoid plagiarism, but overdocumenting a paper is not the way to do it. Overdocumentation is itself a serious error in a researched paper.

Writers should not cite *factual* material that is clearly part of the historical record, or standard body of information, surrounding a topic. Fulfilling this last requirement can be particularly difficult when citing the findings in studies that either are or certainly appear to be fact. For example, a writer would not need to cite a specific study in order to say in a paper *that a person who smokes a pack or more of cigarettes per day is more likely than a nonsmoker to develop heart disease.* Such a statement is part of what we call *common domain*, which means that the idea is so widely held that no one *owns* it. On the other hand, a writer would have to cite a specific study in order to say *that a person who smokes a pack or more of cigarettes per day is 33 percent more likely than a nonsmoker to develop heart disease.* The statistic 33 percent belongs to the researcher who made the study and is the product of the methodology employed by that researcher. The 33 percent figure is not a fact but, rather, a reference to probability; the writer who wishes to use that number must acknowledge the source in which it appears.

A researcher should also use formal citations to acknowledge the use of direct quotations, paraphrases of material that *belongs* to another researcher, and the use of visual presentations of data.

Direct Quotations

Any direct quotation (which means exact language from the source) used in a researched paper or report must have a note to indicate the source and page number of that quotation. Short, direct (fewer than five lines) quotations must also be enclosed by quotation marks. Longer quotations will be set off from the text in block form and will have no quotation marks. In both cases, a note is necessary. Generally, a researcher will choose to quote a source when to do so gives authority to a major idea and when that idea receives complete treatment in a few sentences (three to five).

Paraphrase

Any paraphrase of an idea that gives an opinion, interpretation, projection, or other form of nonfactual material, and that is not part of the *common domain*, should have a source note. Paraphrase means the expression of an idea in language and structure belonging to the researcher. Common domain means that the same basic idea can be found in three or more sources. In the heart disease/smoking example used previously, the fact that smoking increases the risk of heart disease is a common domain idea, whereas the statement that smoking increases the risk by 33 percent belongs to the researcher who derived that probability. A researcher will want to paraphrase when the idea being used can be stated briefly or when the idea is treated in the source in an extended discussion that the researcher can sum up by paraphrasing.

Visual

Anytime a researcher takes the physical form of a table, graph, chart, and so on, from a source and uses that visual in his or her paper or report, a source note is necessary. This same rule does not necessarily apply to the information extracted from a visual such as a table, which can be factual and may not need a citation.

These guidelines for what to document apply regardless of the form of documentation a researcher chooses to use. Every researcher should, however, master at least one documentation style and perhaps be familiar with others. Those described here are representative of styles commonly used in research report writing.

Modern Language Association Documentation Style

For many years, the Modern Language Association (MLA), an organization of language, literature, and linguistics scholars, has published a documentation-style manual. The current style manual, *MLA Handbook for Writers of Research Papers* (1988), is in its third edition and is one of the most widely used guides for citing research available. As the MLA system has evolved, it has developed simplicity, particularly since moving to the use of internal, in-text citations. The *MLA Handbook* is a lengthy volume, and the review provided here is not a substitute. We can, however, examine the basic philosophy and mechanics of MLA citations.

How to Cite Material: In-text notes are just that; they are parenthetical citations placed after the cited material. Generally, the note contains the author's last name and page number: *(Jones 34)*. If a *Works Cited* contains sources by more than one author of the same last name, the note contains the initial and last name of the author and page number: *(A. Jones 34)*. If the Works Cited contains more than one source by the same author, a short form of the title being cited appears: *(Jones, "Antitrust Laws" 34)*. When the author of a source is not named, a short form of the title and page number appear: *("Antitrust Laws" 34)*. When a researcher is citing material from a single volume of a multivolume work, the citation will indicate volume and page number: *(Jones 2: 34)*. When a source has only one page, no page number is necessary: *(Jones)*. Sometimes researchers refer to the name of the author, if the source identifies one, or title, if no author is listed, within the text of their paper or report. In such cases, the note simply requires a page number: *(34)*.

When a source note appears after an in-text quotation, the researcher closes quotation marks, adds the note, then places a period for the end of a sentence: ". . . *all federal cases*" *(Jones 34)*. When a source note appears after a block quotation, the researcher ends the quotation, places a period, then adds the source note:

Antitrust laws are constantly in a state of change, although their basic components remain the same, and they apply in all federal cases. (Jones 34)

In all source notes, the author's name, the title—whatever the researcher is using—must connect the note to the entry for that source in the Works Cited.

Works Cited: A Works Cited is not a bibliography. A Works Cited lists only those researched sources from which material is cited in the text of the paper or report. These sources must be listed in alphabetical order by the first *significant* word in the entry. Usually, this first word is the last name of the author, although, for sources without authors, the first significant word of the title is used.

Works Cited entries take the form of standard bibliography entries. Following are examples of some of the most common types of sources used in research and their format according to the *MLA Handbook for Writers of Research Papers* (1995).

Book by a Single Author

Wilson, Janet. *An Aging Population*. New York: Peterson Publishing, 1986.

Two or More Books (Sources) by the Same Author

Hill, Christopher. *Society and Puritanism in Pre-Revolutionary England*. New York: Viking Penguin, Inc., 1964.

---. *Some Intellectual Consequences of the English Revolution: A Twentieth-Century Perspective*. Madison: U of Wisconsin P, 1980.

A Book by Two or More Authors

Jasper, Dale, and James Darelson. *The Business Index Review*. Atlanta: Southern Associates Publishing, 1992.

Corporate Author and Edition

National Accountancy Associates. *Redefining Deductions*. 3rd ed. New York: Crosby, Inc., 1991.

Work in an Anthology and Editor

Darley, Terry. "The Deficit and Interest Rates." *Issues in American Finance*. Ed. Donald Stang. New York: Patterson and Sons, 1989. 65–78.

Introduction, Foreword, Preface, Afterword

Peters, Darlene. Introduction. *Investing in Mexico*. By J. D. Phillips. Chicago: Haroldson and James, Publishers, 1993. v–xi.

Republished Book

Clark, A. J. *Entrepreneurism*. 1956. New York: Denis Publishing, 1991.

Article in a Reference Book

Masters, Davis. "Productivity." *Encyclopedia Britannica*. 1974.

Government Publication

United States. Dept. of Defense. *1993 Appropriations*. Washington: GPO, 1993.

Article in a Newspaper

Myers, Charles. "Merger Pending." *Wall Street Journal* 10 June 1983, eastern ed.: A1⁺.

Article in a Magazine

Brunswick, Carla. "Finding the Loopholes." *Financial Times* 16 Dec. 1987: 274-75.

Article in a Journal (Separate Pagination)

Ross, Bert. "A Growing Industry." *Midwest Review* 43.3 (1981): 77–80.

Article in a Journal (Continuous Pagination)

Barker, Margaret. "Finding Hidden Value." *Monetary Guide* 25 (1986): 101–26.

American Psychological Association Documentation Style

Like the MLA documentation style, *Publication Manual of the American Psychological Association* (1994) employs in-text notes. These notes and the bibliography forms with which they correlate place particular emphasis on the date of a source. This emphasis accounts for the primary difference between the APA and MLA styles. The differences, however, are significant enough that we need to look at the specific details of the APA style.

How to Cite Material: APA in-text notes provide enough information that the reader can look at the *References* page in the report to know exactly which source the note refers to. The basic in-text note places in parentheses the name of the author, the date of the source, and the page number in the source of the quotation or idea being cited: *(Jones, 1990, p. 26)*. Because the note contains the date of the source, the reader usually has no problem even if the References page lists more than one work by the same author or works by more than one author with the last name. When, however, an author has more than one work published in the same year, the writer will designate these works in both the References and in internal notes as *a*, *b*, *c*, and so on: *(Jones, 1990a, p. 26)*.

APA and MLA style also differ significantly when the name of the author whose work is being cited appears in the text of the report. APA divides the note: *According to Jones (1990), "A forecaster cannot provide reliable analysis without a valid statistical model" (p. 26)*.

At times a researcher will find that several sources make a similar claim and will wish to acknowledge that fact by providing a general citation without page numbers but referring to all the sources. Such a note is structured to give the authors' names and the dates of the cited sources, usually alphabetically: *(Billings and Carson, 1993; Jones, 1990; Wilson, 1992)*.

End punctuation after a note in APA style is the same as used according to MLA style.

References: A References page in a report documented according to APA style is not a bibliography. Only researched sources from which material is cited in the text of the report are listed. These sources are listed in alphabetical order. Following are example APA forms for some of the most commonly used types of sources.

Book by a Single Author

Wilson, Janet. (1986). *An aging population*. New York: Peterson Publishing.

Two or more Sources by the Same Author from the Same Year

Wilson, Janet. (1986a). *Aging and healthcare issues in the sunbelt*. Atlanta: Southern Studies Institute,

Wilson, Janet. (1986b). *An aging population*. New York: Peterson Publishing.

Two or More Books (Sources) by the Same Author

Hill, Christopher. (1964). *Society and puritanism in pre-revolutionary England*. New York: Viking Penguin, Inc.

Hill, Christopher. (1980). *Some intellectual consequences of the English revolution*. Madison: University of Wisconsin Press.

A Book by Two or More Authors

Jasper, Dale, & Darelson, James (1992). *The business index review*. Atlanta: Southern Associates Publishing.

Corporate Author and Edition

National Accountancy Associates. (1991). *Redefining deductions*. (3rd Edition). New York: Crosby, Inc.

Work in an Anthology and Editor

Darley, Terry. (1989). The deficit and interest rates. In Donald Stang (Ed.), *Issues in American finance* (pp. 65–78). New York: Patterson and Sons.

Article in a Reference Book

Masters, Davis. (1974). *Productivity*. Encyclopedia Britannica.

Government Publication

Department of Defense. (1993). *1993 appropriations*. Washington, DC: U.S. Government Printing Office.

Article in a Newspaper

Myers, Charles. (1983, June 10). Merger pending. *Wall Street Journal*, p. A7.

Article in a Magazine

Brunswick, Carla. (1987, December). Finding the loopholes. *Financial Times*, pp. 274–75.

Article in Journal

Barker, Margaret. (1986). Finding hidden value. *Monetary Guide*, 25, 101–26.

Chicago Documentation Style

The MLA style manual discusses the use of numbered notes to cite the source of material used in a research paper or report; however, the standard style manual for such documentation is the *Chicago*

Manual of Style. A Manual for Writers of Term Papers, Theses, and Dissertations by Kate Turabian is also commonly used as a guide to endnote documentation. Students may find that their instructors prefer that they use one or the other of these guides and should be familiar with what they must do to cite their researched material properly.

How to Cite Material: To cite the source of a direct quotation, the paraphrase of an idea that belongs to a specific source, or a visual according to the *Chicago* style, a writer will place a superscripted number, beginning with number 1, after the passage being documented. All subsequent material will be cited in the same manner with superscripted 2, 3, and so on. These note numbers may appear after a word in a sentence (if appropriate): *Arthur Jones says that "irresponsible"[4] is the best way to describe current interest rate hikes;* or at the end of a sentence after the end punctuation: *Jones describes current interest rate hikes as "irresponsible."[4]* Note numbers for quoted material should appear immediately after the closing quotation marks. To review the information on the source for the cited material, the reader will turn to the *Notes* page and find the appropriate note number for the cited passage.

Notes: The Notes page(s) for a researched paper or report should appear at the end of the document and begin on a separate page. The page is headed with the word *Notes* centered. Notes are numbered to correspond to the superscripted numbers in the text. The format for the notes is simple but is also considerably different from the format used for citations on a *Works Cited* or *References* page. Following is a list of sample notes for commonly used sources. Observe, in particular, the different punctuation and spacing these forms employ, compared with the punctuation and spacing for bibliography forms.

Book by a Single Author

1. Janet Wilson, *An Aging Population* (New York: Peterson Publishing, 1986), 23.

A Book by Two or More Authors

2. Dale Jasper and James Darelson, *The Business Index Review* (Atlanta: Southern Associates Publishing, 1992), 456.

Work in an Anthology and Editor

3. Terry Darley, "The Deficit and Interest Rates," in *Issues in American Finance*, ed. Donald Stang (New York: Patterson and Sons, 1989), 65–66.

Introduction, Foreword, Preface, Afterword

4. Darlene Peters, Introduction to *Investing in Mexico*, by J. D. Phillips (Chicago: Haroldson and James, Publishers, 1993), v.

Article in a Newspaper

5. Charles Myers, "Merger Pending," *New York Times*, Sunday, 10 June 1983, sec. 3.

Article from a Magazine

6. Carla Brunswick, "Finding the Loopholes," *Financial Times*, 16 Dec. 1987, 274.

Article in a Journal

7. Bert Ross, "A Growing Industry," *Midwest Review*, 43 (Summer 1981): 77.

Article in a Journal (Series)

8. Margaret Barker, "Finding Value," *Monetary Guide*, 2d ser., 25 (Feb. 1986): 101.

Multivolume Work

9. Craig Sheldon, *The Native South*, vol. 3 of *The Original Americans* (New York: Barker Publishing, 1993), 345.

Bibliography: A report that uses endnotes to cite sources used by the researcher should also have a *bibliography* of sources consulted by the researcher. This list of sources will include works that the researcher did not necessarily cite in the report but that may have influenced decisions such as what constituted *common domain* statements. The bibliography page should be set up with the heading *Bibliography* at the top and centered and with sources listed alphabetically according to the first significant word in the entry, usually the last name of the author. The citation forms them-selves, according to the *Chicago* style, are almost identical to the form employed by the MLA Works Cited page. Any researcher using *Chicago* style documentation should, however, refer to a copy of the manual when constructing both the endnotes and the bibli-ography citations.

Summary

Business research is essentially the same, whether we are prepar-ing a paper for a class assignment or a report for a professional audi-ence. Documentation, however, may depend on circumstances. The style of documentation we employ is generally determined by the nature of our project, the audience for whom our writing is intended, or the norm for a specific discipline or profession. In all cases, how-ever, documentation must be precise and follow exactly the system we have chosen. A lack of precision in our documentation suggests a similar lack of care in our research and analysis.

Exercises

I. **Preparing Citations:** Prepare citations for the following types of sources as they would appear in one of the follow-ing styles: in a Works Cited, for MLA; in a References, for APA; or in a Notes, for *Chicago.* You will find models for some of these entries in this chapter. For others, you will need to consult a more complete style manual for example citations. To do this exercise, you will need to use the library to find a source conforming to the required citation; these are not to be *made up* examples.

1. A daily newspaper article:

2. An article from an encyclopedia:

3. A Movie:

4. An article from a quarterly journal with continuous pagination:

5.   An article from a quarterly journal with separate pagination:

6.   A book with multiple authors:

7.   An article from a monthly magazine:

8.   An essay from an anthology:

9.   An introduction from a book:

10.   An anonymous article from a journal:

11.   One volume from a multivolume work:

12.   A book in its third edition:

13.   A book in translation:

14.   A U.S. government document:

15.   A dissertation or thesis:

16.   A piece of computer software:

17.   Material from a computer service:

II.   **Developing a Bibliography:**   Select from the following topics, and prepare, according to the style manual you prefer, a bibliography of sources. Be sure you use a variety of types of sources, including both books and periodicals: Corporate-sponsored Day Care, Prospects for the Oil Industry, Employee-owned Businesses in the 1990s, Sexual Harassment in the Workplace, The Prospects for Electric Cars, Interest Rates and the Bond Market.

III. **Internal Citations:** What follows is material taken from a researched report, along with the endnotes used to cite references. At each superscripted note, write in the appropriate in-text notes for MLA or APA style. Then use the endnotes to prepare a Works Cited page and a References page for the revised material.

POTENTIAL EARNINGS FROM OIL INDUSTRY INVESTMENT

PROBLEM

During the first four months of 1987, investors saw two decidedly different markets take shape on Wall Street. The market that characterized the first quarter gained approximately 25 percent and saw repeated high-volume days. On the heels of such impressive gains, the Dow Average plunged 94 points in two days of trading at the end of March.

During April, traders seemed unable to decide which market would persist through 1987. On April 3, the market gained 69 points to close at 2390.34. Succeeding days matched this impressive performance, with steady deterioration. On April 21, the market again lurched ahead 66 points to close at 2337.07, still 50 points below the April 3 close.

During the first week of May, the market again seemed to have a full head of steam. On May 1, the Dow closed the week up 50 points at 2286.36, still down 51 points from April 21. Volume for the day stood at 183.1-million shares traded.

Steady declines followed by sudden gains have left investors uncertain and experts scrambling to explain the volatile market. Reacting to April's erratic movement, trade journals have issued statements that fall just short of hyperbole: "The dollar came close to a free fall, and interest rates rose sharply, leaving Wall Street reeling from the bloodbath in the stock and bond markets."[1] Discarding the spice of the above statement, Bartlett accurately sums up the economic factors affecting the market: "Underlying the recent frenzy is the fear that the dollar's fall will trigger higher inflation and double digit interest rates, which would strangle economic growth."[2] To support her claim that the falling dollar is the culprit responsible for the market's activity, Bartlett quotes William V. Sullivan of Dean Witter Reynolds, Inc., "The markets are saying the dollar can't fall any further or we'll jeopardize growth."[3]

Bartlett and Sullivan will find little argument from other investment experts that the dropping dollar and resulting inflation—now
threatening to reach 5 percent in 1987—will affect consumer spending and hurt several major industries. Recent trends already indicate
that consumers are reluctant to buy on credit. Concerning interest
rates, however, the experts are in less agreement. *Business Week*'s Karen
Pennar boldly states, "a determined Fed nudging interest rates now
may be exactly what's needed to stabilize the dollar and bring an end
to the jitters."[4] Peter J. Anderson of IDS Advisory Group, as quoted
by Jeffrey M. Laderman, indicates, on the other hand, "the Fed is not
going to start a global recession to fight a 4 percent inflation rate."[5]
So confident is Anderson that the market will continue to improve—
and that the Fed will not threaten this improvement—that he recently spent the 7 percent cash position of his clients' cash position
on stocks. Thomas B. Stiles of E. F. Hutton, on the other hand, has
recommended that the company's clients reduce their stock holdings
from 75 to 50 percent of their portfolios and increase their cash position from 15 to 35 percent.

FINCO Investment Representatives, Inc., is in the process of evaluating its own investment strategy. Noting that FINCO's clientele is
split between conservative and aggressive investors, W. W. Wade,
Director of Research, has called for a review of all the industries in
which the company maintains holdings for its clients. This report is
on the investment suitability of oil industry holdings for the company's
diverse clientele . . . .

OIL INDUSTRY REVIEW

Impact of Rising Interest Rates

At the end of March, several major banks reacted to the slight
tightening of money by the Fed by increasing their prime interest
rate from 7.5 to 7.75 percent. Just the anticipation of this jump had
caused housing starts to fall 7 percent during the first quarter of 1987.

An increase in the prime can have a major impact on the oil industry, and some increases are inevitable, most experts indicate. Oil
corporations are traditionally some of the most leveraged companies
trading issues on the market. For 1987, Value Line's composite figures indicate that the net worth of an integrated petroleum company

will be $175 billion and that these companies will carry long-term debt of $75 billion, or 42 percent of net worth.[6] In order to deal with the burden of higher interest rates, Standard and Poors says, "[t]hose companies carrying heavy debt loads . . . are being forced not only to reduce staffs and spending, but to sell off assets as well."[7] This reduction in capital only further increases the debt-to-worth ratio. And increasing interest rates could well reduce the exploration by companies already suffering from low prices and feeling no desire to finance operations at high payback and with limited payoff. Such a lack of current activity will only detract from the future potential earnings of the companies and thus their shareholders.

Notes

[1]Sarah Bartlett, "A Bad Case of Nerves," *Business Week*, 27 Apr. 1987, 30.

[2]Bartlett 30.

[3]Bartlett 31.

[4]Karen Pennar, "Jitters! Unsettling Economic Signs Have Americans on Edge," *Business Week*, 11 May 1987, 41.

[5]Jeffrey M. Laderman, "The Correction May Be Just What the Doctor Ordered," *Business Week*, 11 May 1987, 43.

[6]Value Line Inc., *The Value Line Investment Survey* (New York: Value Line Incorporated, 1987), 401.

[7]Standard and Poors, *Oil Industry Survey* (New York: Standard and Poors Corporation, 1987) 17, in vol. 2 of *Standard and Poors' Industry Survey*.

Bartlett article, pp. 30–32; Laderman, p. 43; Pennar, pp. 40–41.

CHAPTER IX

Writing Effective Business Reports

Overview

About the only thing all business reports have in common is that they serve some purpose in a professional setting. That purpose is almost always to provide information, to resolve a problem, or to propose a course of action. We can also safely say that to serve any purpose, a business report needs to be tightly organized. Further generalizations are difficult, however, because of the variety of professional settings and readers for which reports are prepared and the range of problems and actions a company may need to resolve or consider in a report in order to conduct business.

Despite the fact that business reports are often so different, what we can do in this chapter is examine the basic organization and development of an effective report. Our discussion will point up differing strategies for preparing various types of reports. It will also stress the characteristics shared by most reports, regardless of the purpose they serve or the audience for which they are prepared.

Short Reports

Often, letters and memos discuss and resolve problems. Despite the fact that they may be short, when they serve this purpose, they are business reports and need the same qualities that we readily associate with longer documents. In particular, they need a tight pattern of organization identical to the one we find in longer, more detailed business reports. Specifically, a memo or letter report should contain the following sections:

Sections of a Short Report

Define the **Problem** the report is addressing.

Explain the **Method** used to research and approach the problem.

Present **Data.**

Conduct an **Analysis** of the data.

Present **Conclusions.**

Offer **Recommendations** (if appropriate).

In a memo or letter report, one sentence may well fulfill more than one of these requirements, but that sentence will be vital. Consider the following example short report:

JOHNSON MANUFACTURING COMPANY
Internal Memorandum

TO: Mr. Harmon Davis, Purchasing Director

FROM: Jane Phillips, Office Manager

DATE: September 3, 1996

RE: Replacement Desktop Computers

I need to replace five desktop computers for the office staff. Currently, we are using the ADM 486 with a 2 RAM capacity. I'm interested now in increasing our capacity by buying the ADM 486Z with 8 RAM. **This expanded capacity will, however, add $400 to our standard discount price of $1,400.**

I observed the office staff to determine the average time needed to prepare and spell-check one page from a document. ADM's sales representative gave me some information about the expanded efficiency we would have using the 486Z, and I consulted personnel files for salary information.

I am basing my recommendation on the cost-effectiveness of the expanded 8 RAM capacity.

A staff member averages 4 minutes to prepare a document page and 1 minute and 45 seconds to spell-check it. The 8 RAM capacity would cut this spell-check time to 30 seconds. Also, each staff member prepares 64 pages of text per day on average. The increased efficiency of the 486Z would save each staff member 1.3 hours each week. **Since the average salary for the staff is $6.30 per hour, we would save the extra cost of the 486Z in the first year of its three-year cycle.** I, therefore, recommend we purchase the 486Z.

This memo contains each of the required sections of a business report: *Problem*, *Method*, *Data*, *Analysis*, *Conclusion*, and *Recommendation*. We need, in particular, to look at three of these sections and the sentences that develop them:

Problem

This expanded capacity will, however, add $400 to our standard discount price of $1,400.

Method

I am basing my recommendation on the cost-effectiveness of the expanded 8 RAM capacity.

Conclusion

Since the average salary for the staff is $6.30 per hour, we would save the extra cost of the 486Z in the first year of its three-year cycle.

The sentence from the *Method* section is written to identify not sources of information but, rather, the criterion used to judge the proposed action. We call this criterion the *basis of decision*. Now, notice how all three of these *core* sentences have a common feature: They all deal with the issue of *money*. In other words, if the problem is *money*, the approach to solving that problem must consider *money*, and the conclusion leading to a recommendation should come back to *money*. Such consistency is what we call the *unity factor*. This discussion gives us a vital principle of professional writing: *The unity factor is crucial to any business document, be it a memo, letter, report, or proposal.*

Everything we have seen in the memo report would apply to a letter report as well. The only difference would be that the letter would go to a reader outside the writer's professional setting, while the memo would be an appropriate format for sending a short report to a reader within that setting. The basic organization of the report is the same whether it is in memo or letter format. And as we will see, the concept of organization presented here applies to longer reports as well.

From Research Proposal to Final Report

The types of longer reports produced in a professional setting will be as diverse as the settings themselves. Certainly, an engineer preparing a report on bridge construction will not write the same type of report as will an office manager considering solutions to an absenteeism problem. While we cannot dismiss the differences between these two situations or the reports they will produce, neither should we dismiss their similarities. Any report, no matter how long and no matter for what situation, will have the same sections as the memo or letter report we have just examined. Furthermore, each part of the longer report will offer the same type of information contained in a short report, although the information provided will be somewhat more detailed. A *Problem* section, for example, may need to discuss reasons the company is facing a difficult situation or decision; a simple statement of cost, such as we saw in the memo-report example, would be insufficient. A more detailed report might also state several criteria by which an action will be judged, not simply acknowledge the cost-efficiency criterion of our example.

When we speak of a *longer* report, we are suggesting, if not demanding, a report that contains research. Often, in fact, what makes the reports of various professionals *look* different is the type of information they contain and the research the writer has done. The organization of the report and, certainly, the style the writers employ would tend to be the same or, at least, similar.

Throughout this chapter we will look at the research and writing procedure appropriate for a professional preparing a report. To do so, we will define this procedure as follows:

Research and Writing Procedure

Planning a research, analysis, and writing method

Refining that method through preliminary research

Completing the research, **reporting** the findings, and **presenting** a recommendation

---

Each stage in this process has its own professional document: the *Research Proposal*, the *Progress Report*, and the *Recommendation Report*. Professionals who will research and write as part of their jobs must understand how each of these documents should work.

The Research Proposal

With some writing tasks, a *research proposal* is the first document a writer will produce. That initial document will be followed by a final report, often with one or more *progress reports* along the way. In the research proposal, the writer identifies the problem the final report will address, along with the research and writing procedure leading to that report. First, let's look at the heading structure of a research proposal; then we will discuss what each section of the proposal should do. An example research proposal appears in Appendix A, using APA style.

Research Proposal

I. Definition of the Problem

    A. History and Causes

    B. Scope

    C. Possible Results

II. Possible Responses to the Problem

Definition of the Problem

The subheadings of this section make clear what the writer must do: give background on the origin of the company's problem, determine how broad—or how significant—the problem is, and evaluate the possible results of not addressing the problem. In this first section, the writer establishes the significance of the work that will take place. A problem definition also offers the reader the opportunity to react to what the writer is attempting to accomplish, plus a chance to share some ideas before the project moves too far along. The sections on *Scope* and *Possible Results* give immediacy to the writer's project. They may well persuade the reader of the importance of the project, particularly if the writer needs the reader's approval in order to proceed.

Possible Responses to the Problem

Even at an early stage, a researcher needs to have some idea about the best way or ways to research and attack a problem. The research would then become a process of eliminating or refining those options. For example, if a company is losing customers and, thus, revenue, the researcher might look at advertising measures, population trends and location, merchandise, and/or services offered. Several possibilities come quickly to mind, and the nature of the research would depend on what responses the writer plans to investigate. Stating the possible responses early in the process—in the research proposal—is important, because doing so sets the parameters of the entire project.

Criteria for Evaluating Responses

This section may well be the most important in the proposal. In this section, the writer outlines the basis for deciding which possible response to the problem the company should ultimately use. This is the section that dictates the logic of decision making. The writer who is careful with this section will be prepared to focus the research in valuable ways and to make an effective recommendation in the final report.

The first criteria for any decision would be *cost* and *capability*. In other words, can the company afford the response the writer recommends? Does that response really have the capability to solve the problem? In our example about the retailer losing customers, capability means getting people back into the store. So the research would perhaps look at an advertising plan, a possible change in merchandise, or a shift in location with this fundamental capability criterion in mind. Cost might mean considering whether the company could afford to move, could afford the necessary advertising to attract more customers, or could offer a new line of merchandise in order to produce more sales.

Other criteria are possible in addressing the many problems a company might face. Safety could well be a factor in deciding a course of action in industry. So could the legal concerns or government regulations, such as Environmental Protection Agency standards, which often confront industries. We should not limit this section to cost and capability discussions; we simply start with them.

Tentative Sources of Information

Because the proposal is a preliminary document in the research process, the reader would not expect a complete list of information sources. The writer should, however, be able to describe *in detail* a needed experiment, necessary interviews, a survey strategy, and the available written sources that address the needs of the researcher. Certainly, the writer will not be restricted to the listed sources; this initial discussion simply forces the writer to plan the research that lies ahead and to share that plan with the reader.

Researcher's Qualifications

This section of the proposal is optional. A writer is more likely to use it if the proposal is going to a reader not familiar with the writer or the writer's work. Such would be the case, for example, when the writer is serving as a consultant. If used, this section can be treated like a brief resume, in which the researcher makes clear to the reader his or her ability to perform the task or tasks outlined in the proposal. The primary qualifications would be education and experience, especially experience with similar projects.

Budget for Research

The reader will want to know how much the proposed research will cost; in fact, its cost might well determine whether the writer is allowed to proceed. So an item-by-item list of expenses, from hiring a consultant to copying questionnaires, is necessary.

Schedule

Again, in list form, the writer should state, beginning with the date the proposal is submitted, all important dates by which significant steps in the procedure must be completed. Such steps might include when a survey will be conducted, when an interview is scheduled, and when the final report will be submitted.

The Progress Report

The *progress report* follows the proposal at that point in the research procedure where the researcher needs to review the progress made on the project or wants to alter some of the decisions made in the planning stage of the task. Such changes must have some basis in research, so the progress report needs to give preliminary findings. First, let's look at the structure of the progress report. An example progress report appears in Appendix B, with References in APA style.

Progress Report

I.   Project Summary

II. Work Completed

III. Preliminary Findings

IV. Work to Be Completed

V.   Budget for Research

VI.   Schedule

VII.   Works Cited or References

Many of these sections are similar to those presented in the research proposal; the researcher is free to keep anything exactly as it was written for that document or to make changes. However, one purpose of the progress report is to make some changes based on the preliminary findings. Let's look at each section separately.

Project Summary

The purpose of this section is to review information from the proposal but in condensed form. In particular, the writer will again indicate the problem the research is intended to address and the basic approach to finding a solution proposed in that first document. The reader has seen the proposal and needs only enough review to distinguish the writer's project from others the reader also may be following.

Work Completed

This section of the progress report will indicate, in general terms, which of the sources the researcher has examined and which criteria or possible responses have been studied. The section needs no data from those sources or on those criteria. All the writer is doing here is identifying *what* has been done.

Preliminary Findings

This is the section in the progress report where the writer tells what the research has produced. What the writer includes will, of course, be determined by the research that has been completed. So, setting up a rigid requirement for this section is not possible. The data presented should deal with the possible responses to the problem the writer originally set up in the proposal and the criteria for evaluating those responses. However, if the research presented in the Preliminary Findings suggests that new responses or new criteria need to be considered, the progress report allows the writer to make those changes.

Work to Be Completed

As the heading indicates, this section of the progress report will tell the reader what research remains for the project to be completed. The writer will structure this presentation around sources to be consulted, responses to be considered, and criteria to be examined. This section will also mention work to be done based on any changes in procedure that the preliminary research suggests to be appropriate.

Budget for Research

Here the writer accounts for money spent and states the balance left from the original budget.

Schedule

This is the same as for the proposal, except it starts with the date the progress report is submitted and includes any necessary changes.

The Recommendation Report

If the research proposal and progress report have been sound, and the research process they outlined has been followed, the writer will be in a good position to prepare a strong final-recommendation report. Much of what that report contains will follow directly from the previous documents. Again, we would do well to begin with an outline. An example recommendation report appears in Appendix C, with References in APA style.

Recommendation Report

  I. Prefatory Material

    A. Title Page

    B. Letter of Transmittal

    C. Table of Contents

    D. List of Illustrations (if needed)

    E. Executive Summary

II. Definition of the Problem

   A. History and Causes

   B. Scope

   C. Possible Results

III. Research and Analysis Procedures

   A. Sources of Data

   B. Responses Considered

   C. Criteria Used to Evaluate Responses

IV. Findings

   A. Response #1 Evaluated

   B. Response #2 Evaluated

   C. Response #3 Evaluated

V. Analysis

VI. Recommendation

VII. Works Cited or References

You will immediately notice the degree to which this document follows the organization of both the research proposal and the progress report. In fact, the parallel sections are striking. Let's consider each.

Prefatory Material

The need for, and complexity of, prefatory material in a report depends largely on the length of the report itself. The *Title Page* indicates the title of the report, the person(s) to whom the report is submitted, the person(s) by whom it is submitted, and its submission date. The *Letter of Transmittal* follows standard, business-letter format. This letter describes the report being sent (the reasons for its being sent and its content) and documents that the report has in fact been transmitted from the writer to the reader. The *Table of Contents* gives an organized listing of every section (heading) of the report and the pages on which those sections begin. The *List of Illustrations* (if needed) identifies the titles of all graphs, tables, and charts and the pages on which those illustrations appear. The *Executive Summary* provides an abstract of the report with an emphasis on its conclusions and recommendations.

Definition of the Problem

This should appear as in the progress report.

Research and Analysis Procedures

This section is a summary of the sources the writer has used, as anticipated in the proposal and as given for the responses and criteria in the Preliminary Findings section of the progress report. Even in those documents, these were short, descriptive discussions; they should, if anything, be even shorter here. The main thing to avoid is the temptation to provide any data in this section.

Findings

This section provides the body of the report. Here, the writer will give all the important information on each of the possible responses to the problem that the researcher outlined in the progress report. That information should allow the writer to judge the appropriateness of those reponses based on the criteria set up in the proposed research procedure. The writer does want to avoid significant analysis of the researched data in this section. A subheading structure can help keep this focus. Such a subheading structure in a report on our retail-store example might appear as follows:

FINDINGS

<u>Advertising Strategy</u>

Cost:

Capability:

<u>Relocation</u>

Cost:

Capability:

Alternative Merchandise

Cost:

Capability:

With such a series of subheadings, the report will keep its focus. The subheading structure will also help organize the *Analysis* section of the report. All the writer has to do in that section is methodically follow the order of the Findings section and draw appropriate conclusions about the proposed possible responses.

Analysis

Now that the reader has the basic facts, the writer can determine what they mean. *What they mean* should suggest which response is the most desirable. This section may well be simple, if one response is obviously more in line with the stated criteria. When one response is not, the writer is faced with a more difficult and probably more detailed discussion in the Analysis section.

Recommendation

This section may be short, but it is necessary. The writer should not assume that the analysis makes obvious what course of action the report is advocating. In the Recommendation section, the writer should state, specifically, what course of action the company should follow to resolve the problem first identified in the proposal.

Works Cited or References

The whole issue of documentation is discussed in Chapter VII.

Inductive-Order Reports

In the chapter on paragraph organization, we saw that the ideas in a paragraph could be presented in both inductive and deductive order. The same is true for the ideas, or sections, in a report. The pattern of organization presented on pages 166–167 is in deductive order. A report in deductive order begins with introductory material, moves to a data section, and ends with analysis and recommendations. An inductive-order report places analysis and recommendations earlier in the discussion. Such an arrangement of ideas well serves the needs of the busy reader who wants the most important material in a report presented up front. Often, this type of report is called a direct-order or administrative-order report because of the way it is designed to serve a particular type of reader. Following is an outline of such an inductive-order report:

Inductive-Order Recommendation Report

I. Prefatory Material

   A. Title Page

   B. Letter of Transmittal

   C. Table of Contents

   D. List of Illustrations (if needed)

   E. Executive Summary

II. Report Overview

   A. Definition of the Problem

   B. Research Analysis Procedure

   C. Recommendations

III. Findings

   A. Response #1 Evaluated

   B. Response #2 Evaluated

   C. Response #3 Evaluated

IV. Analysis

V. Works Cited

The thing to notice here is that the primary difference between the inductive- and deductive-order report is the arrangement of the material. The sections presented are much the same, regardless of the order. The principle difference is that the inductive-order report opens with the Report Overview section. This section condenses the problem and method discussions from the deductive-order report, in which they received detailed comment. This section contains also the report's recommendations. Putting this discussion in the opening section allows the busy reader to get the necessary context for understanding the recommendations and then to focus on them. They are, after all, what the report is all about. In fact, the rest of the report may receive only limited attention from the busy reader. By providing the findings and analysis, however, the writer has given the reader material to refer to should a question about a recommendation arise. Ultimately, the order in which a report is presented is a tool. The writer must use audience analysis skills to select the best organization for a given situation.

Differences between Long and Short Reports

The discussion thus far has focused on the similarities between long and short reports. Some differences, however, are important:

Comparison of Long and Short Reports

Long reports require a transmittal letter; **short reports** do not.

Long reports require a title page and prefatory material; **short reports** do not.

Long reports are more likely than **short reports** to require formal documentation of researched material.

Long reports will require headings, or at least a more extensive heading structure than will **short reports.**

Long reports need a formal writing style; **short reports** tend to use a personal writing style.

Long reports need more introductory (problem definition and research methodology) material than do **short reports.**

Summary

Technology is changing the business world dramatically, including the ease with which we can research and mechanically prepare reports. Some things, however, have not changed. The basic principles of report organization and development have remained the same despite technological innovation and development. An effective report still needs to establish its context by defining the problem it addresses, as well as the basic procedures used to arrive at a recommendation. It still needs to provide the reader with the data and the analysis of that data that led the writer to specific conclusions and recommendations. Furthermore, all these sections need to be unified, especially those that define the problem, identify the criteria by which a solution to the problem was judged, and justify the conclusions that followed from that judgment.

Exercises

I.   **Selecting Criteria:**   One of the most difficult tasks a report writer must perform is identifying possible solutions to a problem and selecting appropriate criteria for judging those possible solutions. Following is a list of "problem" situations. For each, identify at least three possible solutions a researcher could investigate and as many criteria as are necessary for judging those possible solutions.

1.   A second-year business major needs to buy a desktop computer. The student will use the computer for courses in writing, accounting, statistics, finance, economics, and management. The computer needs to last for at least the student's remaining years in college. Also, the student has to work to pay tuition and living expenses.

2.   A manufacturing business has had two complaints within the past year charging a member of management with sexual harassment. The company has had no policy for dealing with such complaints and has investigated on an ad hoc basis. This situation has made clear the company's need to have a sexual harassment policy in place.

3.   A textile mill in a small, rural town employs more than two hundred workers with preschool-age children and another seventy-six employees who are under age thirty-five. Recently, the only public child-care facility closed. The closure has affected a large number of the mill's employees. Since the closing, the rates of employee turnover and absenteeism have increased dramatically. The cost to the mill in only a short period has been staggering.

II.   **Evaluating a Memo Report:**   Examine the following memo report. Determine its strengths and weaknesses. You will want to determine in particular how well it incorporates and develops the various sections a report needs and the degree to which it maintains unity. Use your analysis to prepare a revised version of the report that does not suffer from the weaknesses you have discovered.

GULF COAST CONSTRUCTION

Internal Memorandum

TO: Mr. Davis Phelps, President

FROM: Janet Barnes, Director of Personnel   JB

DATE: November 13, 1996

RE: New Public Relations Director

You contacted me on October 29, 1996, and requested that I evaluate three internal candidates for the vacant Director of Personnel position. This is a management-level position; unfortunately none of the candidates—Mark Knuckles, Ann Levis, Geri Alisak—has any management experience.

I reviewed each candidate's personnel file and took notice of their previous experience, their record with Gulf Coast Construction, and their ratings from company public relations training seminars. I tried to determine which of these candidates would make the best manager, primarily based on their decision-making ability.

At age twenty-seven, Mark Knuckles has only been with Gulf Coast Construction for three years. He does have an M.A. in journalism and thus has been primarily responsible for writing news releases. His average seminar rating is 83 on a 100-point scale.

Ann Levis has been with Gulf Coast for two years and spent five with Rollo, Inc. Her degrees are in English and advertising, and her seminar rating is 98. Ms. Levis has been responsible for planning and preparing company brochures and manuals.

Geri Alisak has been with Gulf Coast for fourteen years, since completing her associates degree from Regional Technical College. She has assisted the former PR Director as a liaison with local media. Her seminar rating is 92.

Given the length of time Ms. Alisak has served Gulf Coast, I think she is the obvious choice for the new PR Director. She worked with the previous director and should know from that experience what the job requires.

III. **Report Assignments:** Following are several topics for possible short or long reports that will allow you to practice the report writing skills discussed in this chapter. You might also select one of the situations outlined in the first exercise for this assignment.

1. Identify and examine a problem on your campus (registration problem, lack of computer facilities, and so on), and prepare a report for the appropriate administrator recommending an effective response to the situation.

2. Assume you work for a financial-services company that has decided to examine the desirability of including, or excluding, health-care company stocks from its investment portfolios because of the changes occurring in that industry. Select a company—health-care services, pharmaceuticals, and so on—and research whether that company's stock will be suitable for either long-term or short-term investors.

3.   Create a seafood processing company that has recently had an accident involving an employee who works on the processing assembly line and who, during treatment, was discovered to be HIV positive. The company has had no HIV policy but has decided it now needs one in the event of future accidents of this type. Create this policy, taking into account the legal, moral, and public relations issues that would confront the company.

4.   You have received permission from your school to organize a money-making enterprise whereby you will sell a University Consumer Card. The card will allow anyone who buys it (for $10) to shop at a number of local businesses, from fast food to movie theaters, at a 5 percent reduced rate. All you need is financial backing. Prepare a report on how you will market this product for a local business, Financial Services, which provides capital for small businesses. For this assignment, assume your school has 5,000 students. Your ability to secure a loan rests on the strength of the marketing campaign you create.

5.   You are working for the administration at your school. A current concern is the number of students who transfer before they have completed their degrees. The administration would like to know what can be done to retain more students. Prepare a survey that will gather information from fellow students. Your survey should seek the kind of information that will allow you to make specific and concrete recommendations. You can supplement your research by looking at periodical articles on this issue at other schools.

APPENDIX
A

The Research Proposal

REDUCING ABSENTEEISM AND TURNOVER AT COMPTON
TEXTILES, INC., WITH AN ON-SITE
DAY-CARE CENTER

A PROPOSAL FOR RESEARCH

Submitted to:
Mr. Harold Johns, President
Compton Textiles, Inc.

Submitted by:
Lisa Keith, Personnel Relations Director
Compton Textiles, Inc.

February 16, 1996

REDUCING ABSENTEEISM AND TURNOVER AT COMPTON TEXTILES, INC. WITH AN ON-SITE DAY-CARE CENTER

DEFINITION OF THE PROBLEM

HISTORY AND CAUSES

Compton Textiles, Inc., has had an increase in turnover and absenteeism during the past two years. In 1993, the average annual absenteeism rate was four days; that rate has increased to seven days for 1995. The current annual turnover rate is 21 percent, up from 9 percent just three years ago.

Compton Textiles, Inc., loses an estimated $101,550 annually because of turnover and absenteeism. Absenteeism costs Compton an estimated $48,000, primarily through lost production. Turnover costs the company an estimated $53,550, primarily because of the estimated $750 to hire and train a new employee on our equipment.

We can be safe associating most of the increase in turnover and absenteeism with the composition of our work force and the lack of public day care in Sanders, Alabama. Sixty-four percent of our employees have children whose average age is three years, four months. Forty-eight percent of our workers are single; many are single parents. Not coincidentally, I think, the increase in our turnover and absenteeism began in 1993 when the only available local day-care center closed. Personal day care can be so unreliable that employees have to miss days to care for children and so expensive that they prefer to leave work, if possible, and care for their children at home.

SCOPE

A significant number of Compton's employees are potentially affected by day-care issues. Ninety-two percent of our employees are women, and in this region women are still considered to be the parent primarily responsible for children. Many of these women are the head of a single-parent family.

2

Even without these considerations, the fact that 218 of our current employees have children points to the issue of child care, and the additional fact that the average age of our employees is twenty-seven suggests that, if anything, this concern will increase.

POSSIBLE RESULTS

All these statistics point to the fact if child-care problems have led to our increasing rates of absenteeism and turnover, we can only expect these problems to grow. As things stand, the combined cost of absenteeism and turnover is more than $100,000 and approximately 97 percent of the company's current net income. An increase in these operating costs will further cut into the company's already small profit margin.

POSSIBLE RESPONSES TO THE PROBLEM

To combat the problem of no public day-care facilities for our employees and the resulting absenteeism and turnover costs the company experiences, Compton should consider converting its vacant warehouse into an on-site day-care facility. Preliminary research suggests that for $93,000 that building could be converted to handle fifty children. Depending on the potential savings, the company could provide this service to employees at no cost, minimal cost, or full cost.

CRITERIA FOR EVALUATING RESPONSES

The criteria that will be used to evaluate each possible response will be cost and capability. The cost criterion will measure the company's potential savings against the cost to operate a day-care facility. The capability criterion will help dictate potential savings by looking at the degree to which Compton can expect absenteeism and turnover to drop because of an on-site day-care facility.

TENTATIVE SOURCES OF INFORMATION

Following is a list of preliminary sources for researching on-site day-care programs:

Kelly, Tricia. (1992, January). Modern Problems . . . *Quality Progress*, pp. 17–23.

Moser, Cynthia M. (1992, August). The child care business: Should hospitals invest? *Nursing Management*, pp. 50–51.

3

Siwicki, Bill. (1993, November). Pioneering child care center provides parents peace of mind. *Healthcare Financial Management*, pp. 88–89.

Thomas, Linda Thiede and James E. Thomas. 1990. The ABCs of child care: Building blocks of competitive advantage. *Sloan Management Review, 31*, 31–40.

Thornburg, Linda. (1990, August). On-site child care works for health-care industry. *HR Magazine*, pp. 39–40.

Yalow, Elanna. (1990, June). Corporate child care helps recruit and retain workers. *Personnel Journal*, pp. 48–55.

RESEARCHER'S QUALIFICATIONS

I am prepared to conduct the research outlined in this proposal because of previous course work and reports prepared for those courses. I have taken all of the basic management, accounting, and finance courses offered by the School of Business. My Business Policy class required research into the finances of specific companies, and my Management 204 course required a paper on different management styles used in industry.

BUDGET FOR RESEARCH

Photocopies	$6.00
Typing	$18.00
Supplies	$2.00
Mileage ($.28/mile)	$2.52
Total	$28.52

SCHEDULE

February 10	Library trip for research
February 12	Library trip for research
February 14	Proposal to typist
February 16	Proposal submitted
February 19	Library trip for research
February 23	Progress report to typist
February 28	Progress report submitted
March 3	Research report to typist
March 9	Research report submitted

APPENDIX
B

The Progress Report

REDUCING ABSENTEEISM AND TURNOVER AT COMPTON
TEXTILES, INC., WITH AN ON-SITE
DAY-CARE CENTER

A PROGRESS REPORT

Submitted to:
Mr. Harold Johns, President
Compton Textiles, Inc.

Submitted by:
Lisa Keith, Personnel Relations Director
Compton Textiles, Inc.

February 28, 1996

REDUCING ABSENTEEISM AND TURNOVER AT COMPTON TEXTILES, INC., WITH AN ON-SITE DAY-CARE CENTER

PROJECT SUMMARY

The purpose of this progress report is to indicate the status of research on the possibility of using a company-sponsored day-care program to reduce the current rates of absenteeism and turnover costing Compton Textiles, Inc., an estimated $101,550 annually. A significant number of Compton's employees are potentially affected by day-care issues. Ninety-two percent of our employees are women, and in this region women are still considered to be the parent primarily responsible for children. Many of these women are the head of a single-parent family. Even without these considerations, the fact that 218 of our current employees have children points to the issue of child care, and the additional fact that the average age of our employees is twenty-seven suggests that, if anything, this concern will increase. All these statistics point to the fact if child-care problems have led to our increasing rates of absenteeism and turnover, we can only expect these problems to grow.

I have already been able to determine that a free on-site day-care program is not realistic, given the cost-effectiveness criterion. The focus of the remaining research will be to determine the potential benefits of our providing a day-care service at minimal cost to employees. However, I also can see the need to look beyond a simple cost-effectiveness study and to take into account the potential benefit to morale, recruitment, and public image that such a program would bring to the company.

WORK COMPLETED

Thus far, I have consulted only three of the articles I identified in my proposal as having information about company-sponsored day-care programs. These articles have provided me with sufficient information about the cost of such a program and the potential effect it would have on absenteeism and turnover at Compton that I have been able to rule out our providing a day-care service at no cost. A comparison of our potential savings with the high cost of day-care operations simply will not allow us to consider this option further.

2

These articles, however, have shown me that providing day-care services may still be our best approach to solving our current problems with absenteeism and turnover.

PRELIMINARY FINDINGS

Preliminary findings indicate that our company will experience savings from lower turnover and absenteeism costs by establishing an on-site day-care center. These savings do not, however, warrant providing a free day-care service to employees.

Nyloncraft, Inc., Union Bank, and an unnamed hospital organization reduced their turnover rates after establishing an on-site day-care center. Nyloncraft was overwhelmed by turnover problems. After instituting a twenty-four-hour day-care facility, the company's turnover rate dropped to under 3 percent a year. A study conducted by Union Bank found that turnover among their child-care center users was 2.2 percent, compared with a 9.5 percent turnover rate in a control group and an 18 percent rate throughout the company (Thomas and Thomas, 1990, p. 33). The hospital organization, not named in the article, reported that only 2.2 percent of its employees left after taking advantage of the company's on-site center. This company also lost 9.5 percent of employees not using this service (Mosher, 1992, p. 50). If Compton Textiles, Inc., were to enjoy a similar drop in turnover, from 21 percent or 71.4 employees per year, to 3 percent or 10.2 employees per year, the annual savings would be $45,900.

One researched organization also reported reduced absenteeism after establishing an on-site day-care center. According to Mosher (1992), this organization reported that employees using the company's center were absent an average of 1.7 fewer days annually than were employees with children who made other arrangements (p. 50). If Compton's annual absenteeism rate of 7 days per year were to drop by 1.7 days among day-care users, absenteeism will drop by 24.29 percent or 85 days. This reduction assumes that fifty of the company's employees use the facility. Such a reduction creates a savings to the company of $1,728.

The estimated annual savings totals $47,628. Already determined is an increase of $1,400 in insurance, leaving a balance of $33,628 for operating expenses.

3

Preliminary findings do indicate that providing an on-site day-care center will benefit Compton Textiles because the center will reduce turnover and absenteeism costs. Compton will, however, need to charge employees for the service, as the savings are not sufficient to provide operating costs.

Preliminary findings also indicate that intangible rewards are associated with providing a day-care center, benefits such as improved recruitment, strengthened morale, and better public image. Bill Summerlin, senior vice president at Baptist Memorial Hospital, states, "The center now has been open for two years and has proved to be a real plus to Baptist Memorial Hospital's efforts to recruit and retain employees" (Siwicki, 1993, p. 88). David Jansen of Group 243 says the impact on morale resulting from that company's day-care center is apparent: "When you're having a bad day, you just walk over to the day-care center. After spending ten minutes playing with your kids, things at work don't look so bad. Even employees who don't have children in the center walk over to get perked up" (Thomas and Thomas, 1990, p. 32). Clearly, the intangible rewards of establishing an on-site day-care center deserve attention.

WORK TO BE COMPLETED

I have several articles left to review before making my final recommendations about on-site day care. I have yet to determine whether Compton can benefit from providing a minimal cost day-care facility to its employees and what that cost would be. I am also interested in following up on the issues of morale, recruitment, and public image. The research I have completed suggests that company's that provide day care for employees benefit in these three areas. If with further reading I can confirm these benefits, I think we would be well advised to consider them when deciding what course of action to take. Fortunately, the professional journals contain considerable material on company-sponsored day care. After completing this research, I should be able to make detailed recommendations about Compton's situation.

BUDGET

	Budgeted	Used
Photocopies	$6.00	$7.30
Typing	$18.00	$5.00

4

Supplies	$2.00	$0.00
Mileage	$2.52	$1.68
Total	$28.52	$13.98

SCHEDULE

February 28	Progress report submitted
March 3	Research report to typist
March 9	Research report submitted

References

Mosher, Cynthia M. (1992, August). The child care business: Should hospitals invest? *Nursing Management,* pp. 50–51.

Siwicki, Bill. (1993, November). Pioneering child care center provides parents peace of mind. *Healthcare Financial Management,* pp. 88–89.

Thomas, Linda and James E. (1990). The ABCs of child care: Building blocks of competitive advantage. *Sloan Management Review,* 31, pp. 31–40.

APPENDIX
C

The Research Report

REDUCING ABSENTEEISM AND TURNOVER AT COMPTON
TEXTILES, INC., WITH AN ON-SITE
DAY-CARE CENTER

A RESEARCH REPORT

Submitted to:
Mr. Harold Johns, President
Compton Textiles, Inc.

Submitted by:
Lisa Keith, Personnel Relations Director
Compton Textiles, Inc.

March 9, 1996

Compton Textiles, Inc.
123 Commerce Avenue
Sanders, Alabama 23432

March 9, 1996

Mr. Harold Johns, President
Compton Textiles, Inc.
123 Commerce Avenue
Sanders, Alabama 23432

Dear Mr. Johns:

I write to present the enclosed report, "Reducing Absenteeism and Turnover at Compton Textiles, Inc. with an On-Site Day-Care Center." This report is the result of research I have been pursuing for several weeks and postulates a direct correlation between the high absenteeism and turnover rates our company has experienced and the lack of public day care in Sanders, Alabama.

I specifically found that many companies have used on-site day care to address just these sorts of problems. Such companies have not only reduced turnover and absenteeism but also enjoyed enhanced recruiting efforts, employee morale, and public image. I have found that at a minimal charge of $50.25 per week and a fairly modest investment by the company we can in fact convert our current vacant warehouse to such a facility to the benefit of both the company and its employees.

I have enjoyed working with this project and am available to answer any questions you might have after reviewing this report.

Sincerely,

Lisa Keith

Lisa Keith, Personnel Relations Director

Table of Contents

List of Illustrations

EXECUTIVE SUMMARY

For the past few years, Compton Textiles, Inc., has seen significant increases in its turnover and absenteeism rates. This past year, the combined cost of the two was more than $100,000. We see the significance of this loss when we realize that it is equal to approximately 97 percent of the company's current net income. Such losses, combined with my awareness of the number of young and single-parent employees we have, prompted me to examine the effect an on-site day-care program might have on turnover and absenteeism. My research revealed that we are in no position to offer such a service to our employees without charging them for it. I also discovered, however, that the local area has no public day-care facilities, that on-site day-care can reduce such problems as we are experiencing, and that we can offer such a service with a modest investment from the company and at a charge of only $50.25 per week. Given these facts, I have concluded that Compton Textiles should establish a minimal-cost day-care facility and proceed with research to outline implementation plans.

REDUCING ABSENTEEISM AND TURNOVER AT COMPTON TEXTILES, INC. WITH AN ON-SITE DAY-CARE CENTER

DEFINITION OF THE PROBLEM

HISTORY AND CAUSES

Compton Textiles, Inc., has had an increase in turnover and absenteeism during the past two years. In 1993, the average annual absenteeism rate was four days; that rate has increased to seven days for 1995. The current annual turnover rate is 21 percent, up from 9 percent just three years ago.

Compton Textiles, Inc., loses an estimated $101,550 annually because of turnover and absenteeism. Absenteeism costs Compton an estimated $48,000, primarily through lost production. Turnover costs the company an estimated $53,550, primarily because of the estimated $750 to hire and train a new employee on our equipment. Both these figures are higher than the national averages for a textile company our size (see Figure 1).

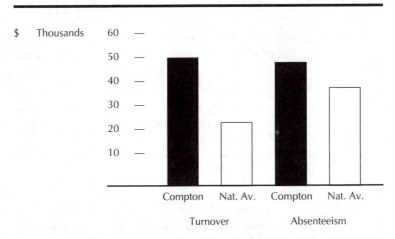

FIGURE 1

Absenteeism and Turnover Cost Comparisons

(National averages are from government statistics and prorated to account for company size.)

2

We can be safe associating most of the increase in turnover and absenteeism to the composition of our work force and the lack of public day care in Sanders, Alabama. Sixty-four percent of our employees have children whose average age is three years, four months. Forty-eight percent of our workers are single; many are single parents. Not coincidentally, I think, the increase in our turnover and absenteeism began in 1993 when the only available local day-care center closed. Personal day care can be so unreliable that employees have to miss days to care for children and so expensive that they prefer to leave work, if possible, and care for their children at home.

SCOPE

A significant number of Compton's employees are potentially affected by day-care issues. Ninety-two percent of our employees are women, and in this region women are still considered to be the parent primarily responsible for children. Many of these women are the head of a single-parent family. Even without these considerations, the fact that 218 of our current employees have children points to the issue of child care, and the additional fact that the average age of our employees is twenty-seven suggests that, if anything, this concern will increase.

POSSIBLE RESULTS

All these statistics point to the fact if child care problems have led to our increasing rates of absenteeism and turnover, we can only expect these problems to grow. As things stand, the combined cost of absenteeism and turnover is more than $100,000 and approximately 97 percent of the company's current net income. An increase in these operating costs will further cut into the company's already small profit margin.

RESEARCH AND ANALYSIS PROCEDURES

SOURCES OF DATA

For this research, I consulted company files to gather information on turnover, absenteeism, and the cost of both to Compton Textiles, Inc. I also reviewed professional, business, and health-care journals, such as *Healthcare Financial Management, Sloan Management Review, Personnel Journal,* and *Employment Relations Today.*

3

RESPONSES CONSIDERED

In the beginning of this research, providing an on-site day-care center at full cost, minimal cost, or no cost were all possible responses to our absenteeism and turnover problem. After preliminary research for the progress report, I eliminated a no-cost facility as a possible option. Clearly the potential savings for the company would not off-set the costs. This report considers the possibility of Compton's operating a minimal-cost or full-cost day-care facility for its employees.

CRITERIA USED TO EVALUATE RESPONSES

Cost and capability have remained the primary criteria for evaluating our possible actions throughout this research. Preliminary research indicated, however, that less-easy-to-measure but also important criteria such as improved recruiting, better employee morale, and public image for the company deserved consideration. I have, therefore, added these criteria to the development of this report.

FINDINGS

CAPABILITY

Research indicates that if our turnover and absenteeism problems are related to the lack of public day-care facilities in Sanders, Alabama, we can possibly reduce our costs from these concerns by 46.9 percent annually, if we provide an on-site day-care center.

Research reports indicate that Nyloncraft, Inc., Union Bank, and an unnamed hospital organization reduced their turnover rates after establishing an on-site day-care center for employees. Nyloncraft had been overwhelmed by excessive turnover problems. Once the company instituted a twenty-four-hour day-care facility, its turnover rate dropped to under 3 percent annually. Union Bank conducted a study that found that turnover among its child-care center users was 2.2 percent, compared with 9.5 percent in a control group and 18 percent throughout the bank's entire workforce (Thomas and Thomas, 1990, p. 33). The hospital organization, not named in this particular article, reported that only 2.2 percent of its employees using its day-care center left the company during the research period, compared with 9.5 percent of employees not using the center who left (Mosher, 1992, p. 50). The common feature here seems to be a turnover rate

4

of between 2 and 3 percent for employees using an on-site day-care facility. If our 21 percent rate were to drop to 3 percent as a result of our establishing such a facility, we would reduce our turnover to 10.2 employees per year at an annual savings of $45,900.

One organization also reports a reduction in absenteeism after establishing an on-site day-care center. This organization, again un-named in the article, reported that employees who use the company's on-site day-care center were absent an average of 1.7 fewer days annually than were employees who made other day-care arrangements (Mosher, 1992, p. 50). If our average absenteeism rate of 7 days per year were reduced by 1.7 days to 5.3 per year among employees using a company day-care facility (one that can accommodate the children of up to fifty employees), we will reduce our current absenteeism rate by 24.3 percent or 85 days. Such a reduction would create an annual savings of 3.6 percent, or $1,728, in absenteeism costs.

The estimated savings in turnover and absenteeism costs would total $47,628. Given that our employees have no public day-care facility, we can conclude that, if anything, our results might be better than those of the companies discussed here. We can also conclude, however, that we would probably enjoy similar results by providing an on-site center at some cost to employees, simply because of the convenience of such a service.

COST

The cost to operate a day-care center varies, depending on geographic location. According to Runzheimer International, a Rochester, Wisconsin management and consulting firm, the U.S. median annual cost for care is approximately $3,564 per child (Sherer, 1993, p. 52). If we were to operate at full capacity (fifty children), our annual operating cost will be approximately $178,200. This figure includes operating expenses such as salaries for child-care staff, food, program materials, and insurance. In addition, we would have an initial expense of $97,000 to convert the company's unused warehouse for this purpose. Even by prorating this start-up expense over five years, to $19,400 per year, we will have then an annual cost to run an on-site facility of $197,600 for the first five years and then $178,200 thereafter. The following table provides a review of costs and potential savings, should the company establish an on-site day-care center.

5

FIGURE 2

Summary of Costs and Savings

Start-Up and Operating Costs:	
Building Renovation (prorated)	$ 19,400
Child-Care Expenses	$ 3,564
Number of Children	50
Total Operating Expenses	$178,200
Total	$197,600
Potential Savings:	
Reduction in Turnover Expenses	$ 45,900
Reduction in Absenteeism Expenses	$ 1,728
Total	$ 47,628
Balance:	$149,972

I think that we can assume the estimated cost figures here to be the maximum the company would face, given that rural Sanders, Alabama, would leave us below the U.S. median numbers. Nonetheless, the balance after savings is significant and suggests that we would have to charge employees for an on-site day-care service.

INTANGIBLE REWARDS

Research indicates that intangible rewards are associated with providing employees with on-site day care, particularly rewards in recruiting employees, employee morale, and public image. Bill Summerlin, senior vice president for Baptist Memorial Hospital, states about his company's program, "The center now has been open for two years and has proved to be a real plus to Baptist Memorial Hospital's efforts to recruit and retain employees" (Siwicki, 1993, p. 88). Summerlin also states, "The availability of the center has resulted in improvements in job performance because parents experience less anxiety, particularly young parents with infants" (p. 89). David Jansen of Group 243 says the impact on morale of that company's on-site day-care facility is apparent. "When you're having a bad day, you just walk over to the day-care center. After spending ten minutes playing with your kids, things don't look so bad. Even employees who don't have children in the center walk over to get perked up" (Thomas and Thomas, 1990, p. 32). Clearly, Compton should consider these potential benefits, as well as the improved public

6

image that several companies have reported, even though such gains are difficult to translate into dollars.

Compton will experience intangible rewards by providing a day-care center regardless of whether we provide that service free or for minimal or full charge. What is once again so obvious in this conclusion is that the lack of a public day-care facility in our community is at the center of our decision.

ANALYSIS

After researching the possibility of providing an on-site day-care center, I have found that Compton Textiles can save approximately $47,628 in absenteeism and turnover costs annually, if we experience the same results enjoyed by other companies that have taken similar action. The estimated annual cost of providing the center will be $197,600 for the first five years and somewhat lower thereafter. The net cost to the company will be $149,972 for the first five years and $130,572 thereafter.

If Compton provides the day-care center to employees at full cost, we would need to charge approximately $58 per child for a week's care, or roughly $3,000 annually in order to break even in the first five years. The cost would drop to $50.25 per child per week, or approximately $2,611 annually to break even after the first five years. Given that the average Compton employee makes roughly $250 per week, these costs amount to between 20 and 25 percent of an employee's gross income.

One option would be for Compton to seek a tax deduction for the cost of renovating its facilities and begin with the lower weekly cost of $50.25 per child. The savings to employees would be approximately $389 per year, sizable enough for us to consider. In fact, were employees to realize the investment the company would make in this effort, they would perhaps better show the improved morale and reduced turnover and absenteeism we are looking to enjoy. Providing the day-care center to our employees at this minimal cost seems, therefore, the better option, as we seek intangible benefits. Also, many of our employees would find the small difference between $58 and $50.25 significant. The $19,000 extra annual cost that I am suggesting the

7

company incur for the first five years of operation is 19 percent of current net income, so my recommendation is not cost-effective in the short term. However, the intangible benefits we would enjoy will likely compensate for the immediate loss.

RECOMMENDATION

I recommend that Compton Textiles move to establish an on-site day-care program for its employees with a weekly per-child cost of approximately $50. The next phase of this research would, therefore, be to prepare an implementation report, beginning with an analysis of Alabama requirements for operating such a facility.

References

Mosher, Cynthia M. (1992, August). The child care business: Should hospitals invest? *Nursing Management*, pp. 50–51.

Sherer, Jill L. (1993, March). No longer a luxury. *Hospitals*, pp. 50–54.

Siwicki, Bill. (1993, November). Pioneering child care center provides parents peace of mind. *Healthcare Financial Management*, pp. 88–89.

Thomas, Linda and James E. Thomas. (1990). The ABCs of child care: Building blocks of competitive advantage. *Sloan Management Review*, 31, pp. 31–40.

APPENDIX
D
Revision

The Three Stages of Revision

Often, writers in business have to produce effective memos, letters, and reports so quickly that finding time to revise is difficult. Revision is, however, an important part of the writing process. Nor are spell-checks or other computer software packages designed to substitute for careful revision or to resolve questions of content and organization. Writers know what they want to say and to whom they are saying it, so only they are in a position to revise effectively.

Effective revision involves a series of steps. The writer wants first to examine a document's overall design, according to the following guidelines:

Revising Overall Design

1. Is the heading structure consistent? Do all main headings look alike? all subheadings?

2. Does the document have any floating headings at the end of a page?

3. Are the page numbers correct and the pages in order?

4. Does the document contain the proper prefatory material?

5. Is all the documentation of researched material in order?

6. Does the document have consistent margins, and do these margins create an attractive appearance?

7. If the document is to be bound, does the left margin leave room?

8. Are all charts, graphs, tables, and so on in the most effective location?

9. Are all charts, graphs, and tables properly designed and easy to understand?

10. Are all the sections of the report in their proper place and clearly marked by descriptive headings?

Next, the writer should reconsider the purpose and reader of the document to be sure that both receive due consideration in matters of organization, content, and tone. The following revision plan can help with these corrections:

Revising for Audience and Purpose

1. Does the document contain all the information the reader needs to follow and be convinced by its conclusions?

2. Does the document contain material that the reader does not need?

3. Is the document organized so the reader can follow its ideas?

4. Does the document contain a summary for the reader with limited time?

5. Does the document contain the proper sections to serve its purpose?

6. Is the document written with the most effective tone?

7. Is the tone consistent throughout the document?

Finally, the writer should revise with close attention to grammar and verb-based language:

Revising Language

1. Do sentences use **it** or **there** subjects?

2. Can sentences that contain passive voice be rewritten to use active voice?

3. Can linking verbs used as main verbs be replaced?

4. Does the document contain weak nouns, especially those ending in ion or ment that can be replaced with strong verbs?

5. Do the verbs in the document need adverbs?

Writers may wish to revise a document three separate times, looking for different types of problems with each reading or to identify and correct the various types of problems that can occur without this type of fragmented revision. The following report contains revisions for all three types of problems. After the revised report is a final version that uses these marked revisions.

AN ANALYSIS OF NEWSPAPER ADVERTISING
INSERTS FOR GAINWAY DEPARTMENT STORES'
WILSON BRANCH

Revise
spacing to
inverted
pyramid.

Submitted to:
Phillip Carson, Operations Director
Gainway Department Stores, Inc.

space

Submitted by
Danny Phelps, Marketing Director
Gainway Department Stores, Inc.

space

February 24, 1996

Omit white
space with
better
layout.

{ AN ANALYSIS OF NEWSPAPER ADVERTISING
INSERTS FOR GAINWAY DEPARTMENT STORES'
WILSON BRANCH

PROBLEM

HISTORY AND CAUSES

The Wilson branch of Gainway Department Stores has
been experiencing a decline in income. From 1987 through
1992, the gross income for the store increased at an average

annual rate of 8 percent. Since 1992, ~~there has been a drop in~~ *the rate of increase has dropped.* ~~that rate of increase.~~ In 1995, the rate of increase was only 1.5 *percent*
and the early numbers from 1996 suggest a continued drop.

In 1992, the year this decline began, Thrift City opened

a branch in Wilson and began high-profile advertising. ~~As~~
Although Thrift City and Gainway ~~you know, Thrift City offers essentially the same merchan-~~ *are similar, the* ~~dise as does Gainway, at comparative prices. The shopping~~ ~~atmosphere is essentially the same as ours.~~ The growth of
the Wilson area would suggest that a second such store could

open without ~~the creation~~ *creating* of this type of problem in income
loss for Gainway, particularly as ours was the established store

~~of the two.~~ During the past, Gainway has not had genuine
competition and thus not advertised. Perhaps the advertising used by Thrift City has created an unequal competition,
demanding that Gainway now initiate a marketing campaign.

This report ~~specifically looks~~ *examines* at the ~~affect~~ *effect* using newspaper
advertising inserts in the Wilson Ledger would have on in-
creasing the visibility of our Gainway branch and the impact
of that visibility on the store's income.

SCOPE

2

Thrift City stores have moved into several markets also served by Gainway. The Wilson branch of Gainway is, however, the only one suffering from such a steep decline in income. I have, therefore, limited my analysis to that branch's ~~situation.~~ *loss of income.*

Vague
wording

POSSIBLE RESULTS

At the current rate of income loss, the Wilson branch of Gainway could well be operating at a deficit within the next two years. ~~If we cannot reverse this trend, therefore, this store will very likely close by 1998.~~ *The store's financial stability may depend on our reversing this trend by 1998.*

Revise to
use more
objective
language.

METHOD

I found several articles on the effect of newspaper advertising inserts on consumers' buying habits. In addition, I conducted a random survey of local consumers to determine their specific use of such inserts when deciding to shop at a particular store. I sent surveys to 200 Wilson residents and received 146 responses. This ~~is~~ *response* sufficient for the *results of the* survey to be valid.

Clarify
meaning
with
precise
language.

The survey asked several questions about general buying habits. The focus, however, was on whether shoppers read newspaper inserts and whether reading them affected their buying habits.

Finally, the advertising sales department at the (Wilson) (Ledger) provided me with ~~information about~~ the paper's circulation and the cost of including inserts in the Sunday paper.

Italicize
title.
Unnecessary
words

Throughout this analysis, ~~there has been a concern~~ *I have been concerned* with whether advertising inserts would generate enough additional sales to pay for themselves, ~~with the assumption that~~ *I assume* if they did the increased visibility the store would receive from them would have long-term, but difficult to measure, benefits.

Omit
"there"
subject.

Use short
sentences
for
emphasis,
and omit
weak noun.

3

FINDINGS

The published material on newspaper advertising does not point to a clear conclusion. George Garneau suggests that for a discount retail store such as Gainway, newspaper advertising is not the appropriate means of resolving problems. ~~It is Garneau's conclusion that,~~ *Garneau concludes,* "the most successful retailers—discounters and warehouse stores that cut advertising costs and pass on the savings by charging lower prices—have posted soaring sales and profits largely without the benefit of newspaper advertising" (~~Garneau~~ 24). Garneau concludes that lower prices, made possible by limited advertising costs, will generate sales much more quickly than marketing efforts in general and newspaper advertising in particular. Garneau also suggest*s* that retailers ~~which do engage~~ *engaged* in advertising campaigns find that inexpensive*,* ~~,~~direct-mail promotions serve as well as do more costly newspaper advertisements ~~(~~ (24)

Garneau's conclusions contrast with ~~The conclusions are not~~ those published in 1985 in (Editor & Publisher) magazine. This article, "The Power of Newspaper Inserts," suggests that newspaper advertising is effective. In one telling finding, this article ~~provides a demonstration~~ *demonstrates* that newspaper inserts are superior to direct-mail preprints for a retailer trying to attract homemakers, an important consumer for Gainway. According to the researchers, "Seventy-seven percent of them said they shopped a store after seeing its newspaper insert versus 62 percent, who said they shopped after reading the mailed preprint" (~~Editor & Publisher~~ *"The Power"* 84). For working women, the number was even higher*,* ~~with the same 62 percent responding~~ *sixty-two percent respond* to direct mail,

Marginal notes:

Omit weak noun.

Omit name from citation.

Maintain parallel verb tense.

Use verbal phrase.

Avoid linking main verb. Italicize title.

Omit weak noun.

Use article title in citation.

4

but a significant 86 percent deciding*e* where to shop after
reading an insert.

Use short
sentences
for
emphasis.

We might explain the different findings of these two articles by examining when the research was conducted. In
1985, the major discounters such as Office Depot and Sam's
Warehouse were not the major players they are today. Their
discounting efforts, ~~which have in many ways shaped our
retail philosophy,~~ may have set the stage for lower price,
rather than advertising efforts, to determine consumer behavior. However, the study I conducted with Wilson-area
consumers provides another possible way of examining our
situation.

Omit idea
that reader
knows
without a
reminder.

The survey I administered to Wilson-area consumers
provided several useful findings. The *main* results of that survey
are presented in the following table:

Clarify
results.

TABLE A Consumer Response to Newspaper Inserts

Improve
text box
title design.

1. Do you shop at general merchandise discount stores?
   Yes: 90%   No: 10%
2. Do you read advertising inserts in the Sunday newspaper?
   Yes: 80%   No: 20%
3. Does reading these inserts affect your decision about
   where to shop?
   Yes: 60%   No: 40%

These results, along with the circulation and advertising
cost I received from the (Wilson Ledger) give us workable

Italicize
title.

5

Avoid repetition.

Omit "it" subject and passive voice.

Italicize title.

Avoid "it" subject and passive voice verbs.

This section lost focus on the purpose of the report and drew conclusions beyond the data.

cost-efficiency numbers. The circulation of the Sunday newspaper is 85,000. Since I limited my survey to respondents who read the Sunday paper, we can conclude that we have the ~~potential of~~ *ability to* attracting 60 percent, or 51,000, of these *potential* consumers with a newspaper insert campaign. ~~It was found in~~ *P*revious studies by Gainway *indicate* that a customer who comes into the store as a result of an advertising campaign generates a $1.50 profit greater than that of "drop-in" customers. With the best possible results, therefore, a newspaper-insert campaign would generate $76,500 less the cost of the campaign. Unfortunately, placing an advertising insert in the Sunday edition of the Wilson Ledger would cost a minimum of $1 per issue or $85,000. ~~It must be assumed, therefore,~~ *We must assume, therefore, that such a campaign would* ~~enough additional income would not be generated by such advertising to cover costs.~~ *not generate enough additional income to cover costs.*

ANALYSIS AND RECOMMENDATION

The findings in the Garneau article, combined with the findings from my survey, suggests that inserts in the Sunday newspaper would not be a productive means of addressing the revenue loss ~~experienced by~~ *at* the Wilson branch of Gainway Department Stores, Inc. ~~Less expensive direct mail could be one effective way of increasing our store's visibility. However, given the conclusions in the Garneau article, I would think that efforts to reduce operational costs which might translate into lower prices would be our best option.~~ *At this point, I could only suggest that we study other possible ways of responding to the income loss at the Wilson branch of Gainway Department Stores.*

Clearly, advertising in the newspaper would only increase such costs without benefit to the store. I must, therefore, recommend we not make that effort.

Appendix D 215

6

WORKS CITED

Garneau, George. "The Retail Ad Revolution and Newspapers." Editor & Publisher November 7, 1992: 24–25.

"The Power of Newspaper Inserts." Editor & Publisher May 4, 1985: 84.

Indent
second
lines.

Italicize
titles.

AN ANALYSIS OF NEWSPAPER ADVERTISING
INSERTS FOR GAINWAY DEPARTMENT
STORES' WILSON BRANCH

Submitted to:

Phillip Carson, Operations Director
Gainway Department Stores, Inc.

Submitted by:

Danny Phelps, Marketing Director
Gainway Department Stores, Inc.

February 24, 1996

AN ANALYSIS OF NEWSPAPER ADVERTISING INSERTS FOR GAINWAY DEPARTMENT STORES' WILSON BRANCH

PROBLEM

HISTORY AND CAUSES

The Wilson branch of Gainway Department Stores has been experiencing a decline in income. From 1987 through 1992, the gross income for the store increased at an average annual rate of 8 percent. Since 1992, the rate of increase has dropped. In 1995, the rate of increase was only 1.5 percent, and the early numbers from 1996 suggest a continued drop.

In 1992, the year this decline began, Thrift City opened a branch in Wilson and began high-profile advertising. Although Thrift City and Gainway are similar, the growth of the Wilson area would suggest that a second such store could open without creating this type of problem in income loss for Gainway, particularly as ours was the established store. During the past, Gainway has not had genuine competition and thus not advertised. Perhaps the advertising used by Thrift City has created an unequal competition, demanding that Gainway now initiate a marketing campaign.

This report examines the effect using newspaper advertising inserts in the *Wilson Ledger* would have increasing the visibility of our Gainway branch and the impact of that visibility on the store's income.

SCOPE

Thrift City stores have moved into several markets also served by Gainway. The Wilson branch of Gainway is, however, the only one suffering from such a steep decline in income. I have, therefore, limited my analysis to that branch's loss of income.

POSSIBLE RESULTS

At the current rate of income loss, the Wilson branch of Gainway could well be operating at a deficit within the next two years. The store's financial stability may depend on our reversing this trend by 1998.

2

METHOD

I found several articles on the effect of newspaper advertising inserts on consumers' buying habits. In addition, I conducted a random survey of local consumers to determine their specific use of such inserts when deciding to shop at a particular store. I sent surveys to 200 Wilson residents and received 146 responses. This response is sufficient for the results of the survey to be valid.

The survey asked several questions about general buying habits. The focus, however, was on whether shoppers read newspaper inserts and whether reading them affected their buying habits.

Finally, the advertising sales department at the *Wilson Ledger* provided me with the paper's circulation and the cost of including inserts in the Sunday paper.

Throughout this analysis, I have been concerned with whether advertising inserts would generate enough additional sales to pay for themselves. I assume if they did, the increased visibility the store would receive from them would have long-term, but difficult to measure, benefits.

FINDINGS

The published material on newspaper advertising does not point to a clear conclusion. George Garneau suggests that for a discount retail store such as Gainway, newspaper advertising is not the appropriate means of resolving problems. Garneau concludes, "the most successful retailers—discounters and warehouse stores that cut advertising costs and pass on the savings by charging lower prices—have posted soaring sales and profits largely without the benefit of newspaper advertising" (24). Garneau concludes that lower prices, made possible by limited advertising costs, will generate sales much more quickly than will marketing efforts in general and newspaper advertising in particular. Garneau also suggests that retailers engaged in advertising campaigns find that inexpensive, direct-mail promotions serve as well as more costly newspaper advertisements (24).

Garneau's conclusions contrast with those published in 1985 in *Editor & Publisher* magazine. This article, "The Power of Newspaper Inserts," suggests that newspaper advertising is effective. In one telling

3

finding, this article demonstrates that newspaper inserts are superior to direct-mail preprints for a retailer trying to attract homemakers, an important consumer for Gainway. According to the researchers, "Seventy-seven percent of them said they shopped at a store after seeing its newspaper insert versus 62 percent, who said they shopped after reading the mailed preprint" ("The Power" 84). For working women, the number was even higher. Sixty-two percent respond to direct mail, but a significant 86 percent decide where to shop after reading an insert.

We might explain the different findings of these two articles by examining when the research was conducted. In 1985, the major discounters such as Office Depot and Sam's Warehouse were not the major players they are today. Their discounting efforts may have set the stage for lower prices, rather than advertising efforts to determine consumer behavior. However, the study I conducted with Wilson-area consumers provides another possible way of examining our situation.

The survey I administered to Wilson-area consumers provided several useful findings. The main results of that survey are presented in the following table:

TABLE A

Consumer Response to Newspaper Inserts

---

1. Do you shop at general merchandise discount stores?
   Yes: 90%   No: 10%
2. Do you read advertising inserts in the Sunday newspaper?
   Yes: 80%   No: 20%
3. Does reading these inserts affect your decision about where to shop?
   Yes: 60%   No: 40%

4

These results, along with the circulation and advertising costs I received from the *Wilson Ledger*, give us workable cost-efficiency numbers. The circulation of the Sunday newspaper is 85,000. Since I limited my survey to respondents who read the Sunday paper, we can conclude that we have the ability to attract 60 percent, or 51,000, of these consumers with a newspaper-insert campaign. Previous studies by Gainway indicate that a customer who comes into the store as a result of an advertising campaign generates a $1.50 profit greater than that generated by "drop-in" customers. With the best possible results, therefore, a newspaper-insert campaign would generate $76,500 less the cost of the campaign. Unfortunately, placing an advertising insert in the Sunday edition of the *Wilson Ledger* would cost a minimum of $1 per issue, or $85,000. We must assume, therefore, that such a campaign would not generate enough additional income to cover costs.

ANALYSIS AND RECOMMENDATION

The findings in the Garneau article, combined with the findings from my survey, suggest that inserts in the Sunday newspaper would not be a productive means of addressing the revenue loss at the Wilson branch of Gainway Department Stores, Inc. At this point, I could only suggest that we study other possible ways of responding to the income loss at the Wilson branch of Gainway Department Stores. Clearly, advertising in the newspaper would only increase such costs without benefit to the store. I must, therefore, recommend we not make that effort.

WORKS CITED

Garneau, George. "The Retail Ad Revolution and Newspapers." *Editor & Publisher* November 7, 1992: 24–25.

"The Power of Newspaper Inserts." *Editor & Publisher* May 4, 1985: 84.

Index